THE WORKS OF SHAKESPEARE

EDITED FOR THE SYNDICS OF THE
CAMBRIDGE UNIVERSITY PRESS

BY

SIR ARTHUR QUILLER-COUCH
AND   JOHN DOVER WILSON

MIDSUMMER NIGHT'S DREAM

A MIDSUMMER-NIGHT'S DREAM

CAMBRIDGE

AT THE UNIVERSITY PRESS

1968

PUBLISHED BY
THE SYNDICS OF THE CAMBRIDGE UNIVERSITY PRESS

Bentley House, 200 Euston Road, London, N.W. 1
American Branch: 32 East 57th Street, New York, N.Y. 10022

First edition 1924
Reprinted 1940
1949
1960
1964
First paperback edition 1968

First printed in Great Britain at the University Press, Cambridge
Reprinted in Great Britain by Hazell Watson & Viney Ltd,
Aylesbury, Bucks

CONTENTS

CONTENTS

A MIDSUMMER-NIGHT'S DREAM

I

Signor Croce says of *A Midsummer-Night's Dream* that 'the little drama seems born of a smile'—and, we may add, 'of a Sunday'—if the old proverb be true that 'a Sunday's child is full of grace.' It is sister, in a fashion, to *Love's Labour's Lost*; but a wiser, more beautiful sister, and with far fewer briars around the palace, for editor or reader. To the approaching lover she seems at first to present a stout hedge for entanglement. To misquote Dogberry, she has two Quartos and everything handsome about her. But in her, as in Silvia,

> beauty lives with kindness.

There is small trouble over the text of this play, and nothing—unless we choose to make it more—to worry us about 'origins.'

II

The story of the text—with which, according to our custom, we deal in a separate chapter—runs simply enough for our purpose in this Introduction. There are two known Quartos, both bearing the date 1600 on their title-pages. The one, usually known as Q_1, was entered to the publisher, Thomas Fisher, in the Register of the Stationers' Company in that year.

The second, which bears the name of James Roberts on its title-page, was not entered in the Register. For long there was never a doubt that this Second Quarto belonged to the date it advertised: until the researches of Greg and Pollard—working on minutiae, including water-marks—conclusively established that the date 1600 is fraudulent and that the book belongs to 1619, having been designed in that year to make one of a set of collected plays[1]. For all this it was from the Second Quarto that Jaggard set up the play in the 1623 Folio.

III

For the date of its composition and first performance, all we can say for certain (for it really amounts to all we know) is that the invaluable Meres mentions it in his list of 1598, or two years earlier than Fisher's Quarto. Speculation has of course run riot over internal evidence —for example over Titania's description (in 2.1.82–114) of her bicker with Oberon and its results in perverting the weather with lamentable effect on the crops.

> And never, since the middle summer's spring,
> Met we on hill, in dale, forest, or mead,
> By pavéd fountain, or by rushy brook,
> Or in the beachéd margent of the sea,
> To dance our ringlets to the whistling wind,
> But with thy brawls thou hast disturbed our sport.
> Therefore the winds, piping to us in vain,
> As in revenge, have sucked up from the sea
> Contagious fogs: which falling in the land,
> Hath every pelting river made so proud,
> That they have overborne their continents.
> The ox hath therefore stretched his yoke in vain,
> The ploughman lost his sweat, and the green corn
> Hath rotted ere his youth attained a beard:
> The fold stands empty in the drownéd field.
> The crows are fatted with the murrion flock,
> The nine men's morris is filled up with mud,
> And the quaint mazes in the wanton green
> For lack of tread are undistinguishable...etc.

'The confusion of seasons here described,' wrote Steevens in 1773, 'is no more than a poetical account of the weather which happened in England about the

---

[1] A.W. Pollard, *Shakespeare Folios and Quartos*, 1909, etc.

time when this play was published. For this information
I am indebted to chance, which furnished me with a
few leaves of an old meteorological history.' This
assertion concerning the weather in or about 1600
Steevens repeated in 1778 and again in 1785; but eight
years later, in 1793 having assured himself that *A Midsummer-Night's Dream* must go back at least so far as
1598 (Meres' date) he calmly shifted back his 'old
meteorological history' some eight years earlier with the
airy statement that his 'few leaves' referred to the weather
'about the time the play was written.' Such are the
licences allowed itself by scholarly conjecture[1]!

Other guesses to be reasonably extracted from internal
study of our play are (1) that Oberon's words in the
same Scene—

> That very time I saw—but thou couldst not—
> Flying between the cold moon and the earth,
> Cupid all armed: a certain aim he took
> At a fair Vestal, thronéd by the west,
> And loosed his love-shaft smartly from his bow,
> As it should pierce a hundred thousand hearts:
> But I might see young Cupid's fiery shaft
> Quenched in the chaste beams of the wat'ry moon:
> And the imperial Vot'ress passéd on,
> In maiden meditation, fancy-free...

—may, or may not, glance at some defeated foreign
political attempt upon the hand of our Virgin Queen.
More certain (2) is our conviction, which grows as we
read, that, at whatever date written, *A Midsummer-Night's
Dream* was composed to celebrate a marriage—possibly
for private performance at some great house, possibly
even at Court, but most certainly for a wedding somewhere. If only we could fasten on the date of some noble
marriage in or before 1598 and link up *A Midsummer-*

---

[1] Nevertheless, it now seems generally accepted and (to
us) highly probable that the bad weather Titania speaks of
belonged to the year 1594 (v. Note on the Copy, pp. 95–6).

Night's Dream to it, we have the date of one performance clinched. In 1598, indeed, Shakespeare's Earl of
Southampton espoused his darling Mistress Vernon, to
whom he had long been betrothed. If we had any
certainty linking the play to that espousal, all would
indeed be well and clear. Certainty is denied us here
as elsewhere; but that there are at least possibilities in
the Southampton wedding a reference to our Note on
the Copy will show. In any event, the play must have
been intended for *some* courtly marriage. It has all the
stigmata. Like *Love's Labour's Lost* and *The Tempest* it
contains an interlude: and that interlude—Bully Bottom's
Pyramus and Thisbe—is designed, rehearsed, enacted,
for a wedding. Can anyone read the opening scene, or the
closing speech of Theseus, and doubt that the occasion
was a wedding? Be it remembered, moreover, how
the fairies dominate the play; and how constantly and
intimately fairies were associated with weddings by our
Elizabethan ancestors, their genial favours invoked, their
possible malign caprices prayed against. Let us take
a stanza from Spenser's *Epithalamion*:

> Let no deluding dreames, nor dreadfull sights
> Make sudden sad affrights;
> Ne let house-fyrës, nor lightnings helpelesse harmes,
> Ne let the Poukę, nor other evill sprights,
> Ne let mischivous witches with theyr charmes,
> Ne let hob Goblins, names whose sence we see not,
> Fray us with things that be not:
> Let not the shriech Oule nor the Storke be heard,
> Nor the night Raven that stil! deadly yels;
> Nor damnéd ghosts, cald up with mighty spels,
> Nor griesly vultures, make us once affeard:
> Ne let th'unpleasant Quyre of Frogs still croking
> Make us to wish theyr choking.
> Let none of these theyr drery accents sing;
> Ne let the woods them answer, nor theyr eccho ring.

Let this be set alongside the fairies' last pattering ditty
in our play:

Now the wasted brands do glow,
  Whilst the screech-owl, screeching loud,
Puts the wretch that lies in woe
  In remembrance of a shroud.
Now it is the time of night,
  That the graves, all gaping wide,
Every one lets forth his sprite,
  In the church-way paths to glide.
And we fairies, that do run
  By the triple Hecate's team,
From the presence of the sun,
  Following darkness like a dream,
Now are frolic: not a mouse
Shall disturb this hallowed house....
I am sent with broom before,
To sweep the dust behind the door.

*   *   *

To the best bride-bed will we:
Which by us shall blessèd be:

*   *   *

And each several chamber bless,
Through this palace, with sweet peace.

Can anyone set these two passages side by side and
doubt *A Midsummer-Night's Dream* to be intended for
a merry κάθαρσις, a pretty purgation, of those same
goblin terrors which Spenser would exorcise from the
bridal chamber? For our part we make little doubt that
Shakespeare had Spenser's very words in mind as he
wrote.

IV

In dealing with Shakespeare we should respect the
preoccupations of other students, and the allurements
they find in him, however wide of our own interest or
taste. Johnson's manly words on this point cannot be
too constantly borne in mind by any actual or prospective
Shakespearian scholar.—

I can say with great sincerity of all my predecessors, what
I hope will hereafter be said of me, that not one has left

Shakespeare without improvement, nor is there one to whom I have not been indebted for assistance and information.... They have all been treated by me with candour, which they have not been careful of observing to one another. It is not easy to discover from what cause the acrimony of a scholiast can naturally proceed. The subjects to be discussed by him are of very little importance; they involve neither property nor liberty; nor favour the interest of sect or party. The various readings of copies, and different interpretations of a passage seem to be questions that might exercise the wit without engaging the passions.

Let us observe Johnson's spirit in dealing with the subject that comes next to our hand—the alleged 'sources' of *A Midsummer-Night's Dream*. Concerning Shakespeare's 'sources' we must, of course, discriminate. When, for example, he borrows from North's *Plutarch* he keeps as a rule extremely close to the prose story, even to the prose text—converting it into noble poetry by the most dexterous, most economical touches. Nay, so deeply absorbed is he in his original that now and again (but oftenest perhaps in *Julius Caesar*) he omits something which *he* remembers from Plutarch—just forgets, or has forgotten, to put it in—and leaves some stray speech or allusion dangling in the air, to puzzle us until we turn to Plutarch and discover its relevance. With Holinshed he takes far wider liberties: yet we can usually go to Holinshed, seek out the original passage and know where we are. Or again in *As You Like It* we know on what he is building: it is Lodge's novel *Rosalynde, Euphues' Golden Legacie*, and we can see just what he makes of it. But it is quite 'other guess-work' when we come to the *Dream* or *The Tempest* (both of which plays take us into fairy-land). So far as anyone has been able to discover—and considering the amount of pains spent by curious minds in tracking Shakespeare to his 'sources' we take that qualification to be no mean one—in these plays he was building on no other man's plot. No author, to be sure, can build *in*

vacuo, fetching his bricks from nowhere, and Mr Frank
Sidgwick has brought together in a small volume[1], and
discussed, the sources or (as he puts it alternatively and
better) the analogues, which may have been running in
Shakespeare's mind as he wrote this fantasy of the *Dream*.
The story, as he points out, is woven of three threads,
which we can disentangle with ease into (1) the main,
sentimental, plot of the court of Theseus and the four
lovers, (2) the grotesque, buffooning plot of Bottom and
his fellows, with the interlude of *Pyramus and Thisbe*,
and (3) the fairy plot. For the first, Shakespeare may
have used floating hints from Chaucer's *Knightes Tale*
of Palamon and Arcite, afterwards the set theme of
The Two Noble Kinsmen: and from North's Plutarch's
Life of Theseus. For the second, Ovid includes the
legend of Pyramus and Thisbe in the 4th Book of his
Metamorphoses, and we know that Shakespeare knew his
Ovid—if not, as many contend, in the original, at any
rate in Arthur Golding's translation (1575). For the
third, Mr Sidgwick can, of course, quote his fairy songs
in abundance: songs about Robin Goodfellow—

> From Oberon in fairy land,
>   The king of ghosts and shadows there,
> Mad Robin I, at his command
>   Am sent to view the night-sports here...
>
> By wells and rills, in meadows green,
>   We nightly dance our heyde-guys;
> And to our fairy King and Queen
>   We chant our moonlight minstrelsies.
>   When larks 'gin sing,
>   Away we fling:
>   And babes new-born steal as we go,
>   And elf in bed
>   We leave instead
>   And wend us laughing, *ho, ho, ho!*

[1] *The Sources and Analogues of 'A Midsummer-Night's
Dream.'* Compiled by Frank Sidgwick. London, 1908.

—and so, through Bishop Corbett's

> Farewell rewards and Fairies!

—to Thomas Campion's

> Hark, all you ladies that do sleep!
>   The fairy queen, Proserpina,
> Bids you awake and pity them that weep.
>   You may do in the dark
>   What the day doth forbid.
>   Fear not the dogs that bark,
>   Night will have all hid....
>
> In myrtle arbours on the downs
>   The fairy queen, Proserpina,
> This night by moonshine leading merry rounds,
>   Holds a watch with sweet Love,
>   Down the dale, up the hill,
>   No plaints or groans may move
>   Their holy vigil....[1]

But may we suggest that while these and other strains
may have been singing in Shakespeare's head while
he wrote, it is even more likely that he brought all
this fairy-stuff up to London in his own head, packed
with nursery legends of his native Warwickshire?
When will criticism learn to allow for the enormous
drafts made by creative artists such as Shakespeare
and Dickens upon their childhood? They do not, as
Wordsworth did, write it all out in a story and call it
The Prelude: but surely they use it none the less.

V

If this be true, may it not be just as true and as
scientific a way of getting at the meaning of *A Midsummer-
Night's Dream* if we try (in all modesty) to get at the

[1] Campion's song did not see print, so far as we know,
until published in his (first) *Booke of Ayres, Set foorth to be
song to the Lute, Orpherion and Base Viol, by Philip Rosseter,
Lutenist,* 1601.

workings of Shakespeare's mind and reason them out more or less in the following fashion[1]?—

Here (say we) we have a young playwright commissioned to write a wedding-play—a play to be presented in some great private house before a distinguished company. He has patrons to conciliate, favour to win, his own ambitions to set in a fair road of success. He is naturally anxious to shine; here is his opportunity; and, moreover, though his fellow-playwrights already pay him the compliment of being a little jealous, he still has his spurs to win. '*Upstart crow* am I? You wait a bit, my supercilious University wits, and see what a countryman can make, up from Warwickshire.'

He turns over his repertory of notions, and takes stock. 'I must not repeat the experiment of *Love's Labour's Lost*. Lyly's model has had its day; the bloom is off it, even for travesty; and that was a witty topical play with malice in it. One must not introduce topical hits or malice in celebrating a bridal....I have shown that I can do great things with the trick of mistaken identity, but I cannot possibly push the fun of it farther than I did in *The Comedy of Errors*; and the fun there, which I stole from Plautus, was clever but a trifle hard, inhuman...not at all the thing for a wedding....A wedding, if any occasion on earth, should be human: what is more, a wedding above any occasion on earth calls for poetry—and I *can* write poetry—witness my *Venus and Adonis*....Still, mistaken identity is a trick I know, a trick at which I am known to shine....If I could only make it poetical!...A pair of lovers, now?... For mistaken identity, *that* means *two* pairs of lovers,

---

[1] The mere speculations that follow are taken, with permission, from *Shakespeare's Workmanship* (T. Fisher Unwin, 1918), a series of lectures given at Cambridge. They profess to be no better than a tentative step—easily discredited— in a somewhat new method of interpretation. 'The worst are no worse, if imagination amend them.'

mischanging oaths somehow....Yet I must on no account make it farcical. It was all very well, in *Errors*, to make wives mistake their husbands. That has been funny ever since the world began; and as ancient as cuckoldry, or almost. But this is a wedding-play, and the sweethearting must be fresh. Lover and Beloved are not so easily mistaken, deluded, as wife and husband —or ought not to be—in poetry.

'I like, too'—we fancy the young dramatist continuing—'this situation of the scorned lady following her love....I did not quite succeed with it in *The Two Gentlemen of Verona*: but it is a good situation, nevertheless. Can I use it again[1]?...

'Lovers mistaking one another...scorned lady following the scorner, wandering...through a wood, say... Yes, and by night: this has to be written for a bridal eve....

'A night for lovers—a warm night—a summer's night —a midsummer's night—dewy thickets—the moon.... The moon? Why, of course, the moon! Pitch darkness is for tragedy, moonlight for love, for illusion. Lovers can be pardonably mistaken—under the moon....What else—on a summer's night, in woodland, under the moon?

'Eh?...Oh, by Heaven! Fairies! Fairies, of course! Yes, and real Warwickshire fairies! Fairies full of mischief—and for a wedding, too! How does that verse of Spenser go?—

> Ne let the Pouke...

Fairies, artificers and ministers of all illusion...the fairy ointment, philtres, pranks...fairies that

> take the shining metals
> And beat them into shreds;
> And mould them into petals
> To make the flowers' heads,

---

[1] And he did: not only in this play, but in *All's Well That Ends Well*. It has a beautiful reflex in *Cymbeline*.

and, crown of their hammering, the little western
flower

> Before, milk-white; now purple with love's wound—
> And maidens call it, Love-in-idleness.

These, and wandering lovers, a mistress scorned—Why,
we scarcely need the moon after all!'

Then—for Shakespeare's fancy never started to work
but it forthwith teemed—one can watch it opening out
new alleys of fun, weaving its delicate filigrees upon
and around the central invention. 'How, for a tangle,
to get one of the fairies caught in the web they spin?
Why not even the Fairy Queen herself?...Yes; but the
mortal she falls in love with? Shall he be one of the
lovers?...Well, to say the truth, I have not given any
particular character to those lovers. The absolute jest
would be to introduce opposite extremes upon the
middle illusion of the stage lovers, to make the Queen of
Fairies herself dote on a gross clown—say through some
overreaching cleverness of Puck's....All very well, but
I haven't any clowns!

'The answer to *that* is, If I haven't I ought to have....
Stay again! I have been forgetting the Interlude all
this while. An Interlude is expected in a wedding-play.
...Now suppose we make a set of clowns perform the
Interlude—an improvement upon the eccentrics in
Love's Labour's Lost, and get them chased by the fairies
while they are rehearsing? Gross flesh and gossamer—
that's an idea! If I cannot use it now I certainly will
some day[1]....But I *can* use it now! What is that story
in Ovid about Midas and the ass's ears? Or am I
confusing it with a story I read the other day, in a book
about witches, of a man transformed into an ass?'[2]

Ohe! jam satis! Nobody suggests, of course, that
Shakespeare hammered out *A Midsummer-Night's
Dream* just in that way. Yet is it likely to be a nearer

---

[1] He did: in 5. 5. of the *Wives*.   [2] See p. 168.

guess at his operation than any that can be reached by the traditional conception of a shadowy Prospero plucking out this or that volume from his library in search for his next plot? Admittedly Shakespeare was by habit careless whence he took his themes; and admittedly the plot of *A Midsummer-Night's Dream* is fairly ingenious. But why on earth people who, for the rest, idolise the man—why on earth they must choose to doubt him in one respect so lacking in ingenuity that he *could* never have written a drama without filching the idea of it from some inferior, British or foreign, baffles understanding. A man so opulent of imagination and of words and music and emotion and all other gifts of great poetry to be so confidently assumed a needy beggar of invention!

VI

The play, at any rate, contains three plots: and these three plots are so prettily interwoven as to provide us not only with an early confutation of Ben Jonson's dictum, reported by Drummond of Hawthornden, that Shakespeare 'wanted art,' but with a help to discover the stage of his career at which he found himself as an artist. We cannot, needless to say, fix that moment for a genius so mighty in operation as Shakespeare's—

> For while the tired waves, vainly breaking,
> Seem here no painful inch to gain,
> Far back, through creeks and inlets making,
> Comes silent, flooding in, the main.

There must have been, after all, a tide in Shakespeare that gathered and swelled and carried him up from *The Two Gentlemen of Verona* to *Twelfth Night*, from *The Comedy of Errors* to *The Tempest*, as from *Titus Andronicus* to *Hamlet*, from *Richard the Third* or *Romeo and Juliet* to *Antony and Cleopatra*. And we can say of *A Midsummer-Night's Dream* that here is a thing Shakespeare could not do when he was writing *The*

Two Gentlemen of Verona. He has mastered the trick of it. As Mr Max Beerbohm once said in effect, writing on a performance of this play, 'Here we have the Master, confident in his art, at ease with it as a man in his dressing-gown, kicking up a loose slipper and catching it on his toe.' *A Midsummer-Night's Dream* shows a really careless grace—the best grace of the Graces.

Critics have complained that he gets his effect at the expense of stagifying his quartet of lovers—Lysander, Demetrius, Hermia, Helena—depriving them of separate character. But the complaint is not over-intelligent. In the first place, he does get his effect—which is something. Secondly the play is a Dream, and in a dream reality and fantasy are allowed to exchange places : nay, it is a part of the illusion that they should. To shift Theseus' words to these Athenian lovers 'the best in *this* kind are but shadows'—in a magic wood where Oberon reigns and has a real quarrel with his queen—'and the worst are no worse, if imagination amend them.' Love, mortal love—'fancy,' as the Elizabethans called it—is a craze, a passion bred nor in the heart nor in the head. 'Let us all ring fancy's knell'—in this magic wood where the fairies are wise, and the mortals all, in one way or another, demented—'Lord, what fools these mortals be!'

VII

We feel, at any rate, reading this play as it has come to us, that Shakespeare at last is pulling out the stops for his full music—not only his native wood-notes wild

> I know a bank where the wild thyme blows,
> Where oxlips and the nodding violet grows,
> Quite over-canopied with luscious woodbine,
> With sweet musk-roses, and with eglantine:
> There sleeps Titania, some time of the night,
> Lulled in these flowers...

or   The honey-bags steal from the humble-bees,
        And for night-tapers crop their waxen thighs,
        And light them at the fiery glow-worm's eyes,
        To have my love to bed and to arise...

[imitated, of course, by Herrick, in his *Night-piece:
to Julia*:

        Her eyes the glow-worm lend thee,
        The shooting stars attend thee;
            And the elves also,
            Whose little eyes glow
        Like the sparks of fire, befriend thee...]

or   Never so weary, never so in woe,
        Bedabbled with the dew and torn with briars,

but the deeper-toned phrases such as

        Following darkness like a dream,

or   And as imagination bodies forth
        The forms of things unknown, the poet's pen
        Turns them to shapes, and gives to airy nothing
        A local habitation and a name.

That is just what this, the spirit, fairy-tale does—

        Cras amet qui nunquam amavit—

before out of the humid midsummer wood, which it
has drenched with poetry, it nestles like Ariel on the
bat's back and escapes us, 'following darkness like a
dream.' But the lark will be up 'from his moist cabinet.'
and Autolycus will wake under the hedge to watch it.

        The lark, that tirra-lirra chants
            With heigh! with heigh! the thrush and the jay—
        Are summer songs for me and my aunts,
            While we lie tumbling in the hay.

VIII

One of the editors once discussed with a friend how,
if given their will, they would have *A Midsummer-Night's
Dream* presented. They agreed at length on this:

The set scene should represent a large Elizabethan hall, panelled, having a lofty oak-timbered roof and an enormous staircase. The cavity under the staircase, occupying in breadth two-thirds of the stage, should be fronted with folding or sliding doors, which, being opened, should reveal the wood, recessed, moonlit, with its trees upon a flat arras or tapestry. On this secondary remoter stage the lovers should wander through their adventures, the fairies now conspiring in the quiet hall under the lantern, anon withdrawing into the woodland to befool the mortals straying there. Then, for the last scene and the interlude of *Pyramus and Thisbe*, the hall should be filled with lights and company. That over, the bridal couples go up the great staircase. Last of all—and after a long pause, when the house is quiet, the lantern all but extinguished, the hall looking vast and eerie, lit only by a last flicker from the hearth— the fairies, announced by Puck, should come tripping back, swarming forth from cupboards and down curtains, somersaulting downstairs, sliding down the baluster rails; all hushed as they fall to work with their brooms— hushed, save for one little voice and a thin, small chorus scarcely more audible than the last dropping embers:

> Through the house give glimmering light,
>   By the dead and drowsy fire,
> Every elf and fairy sprite
>   Hop as light as bird from briar....
> Hand in hand, with fairy grace,
> Will we sing and bless this place....

>   Trip away:
>   Make no stay:
> Meet me all by break of day

—and this is, we conceive, not far from picturing the play as it was actually presented in 1598[1].

Q.

[1] v. pp. 98, 151.

TO THE READER

The following is a brief description of the punctuation and other typographical devices employed in the text, which have been more fully explained in the *Note on Punctuation* and the *Textual Introduction* to be found in *The Tempest* volume:

An obelisk (†) implies corruption or emendation, and suggests a reference to the Notes.

A single bracket at the beginning of a speech signifies an 'aside.'

Four dots represent a *full-stop* in the original, except when it occurs at the end of a speech, and they mark a long pause. Original *colons* or *semicolons*, which denote a somewhat shorter pause, are retained, or represented as three dots when they appear to possess special dramatic significance. Similarly, significant *commas* have been given as dashes.

Round brackets are taken from the original, and mark a significant change of voice; when the original brackets seem to imply little more than the drop in tone accompanying parenthesis, they are conveyed by commas or dashes.

In plays for which both Folio and Quarto texts exist, passages taken from the text not selected as the basis for the present edition will be enclosed within square brackets. Lines which Shakespeare apparently intended to cancel, have been marked off by frame-brackets.

Single inverted commas (' ') are editorial; double ones (" ") derive from the original, where they are used to draw attention to maxims, quotations, etc.

The reference number for the first line is given at the head of each page. Numerals in square brackets are placed at the beginning of the traditional acts and scenes.

A Midſommer nights dreame.

As it hath beene ſundry times pub-
lickely acted, *by the Right honoura-*
ble, the Lord Chamberlaine his
ſeruants.

Written by William Shakeſpeare.

¶ Imprinted at London, for *Thomas Fiſher*, and are to
be ſoulde at his ſhoppe, at the Signe of the White Hart,
in *Fleeteſtreete*. 1600.

Scene: Athens, and a wood hard by

CHARACTERS IN THE PLAY

THESEUS, *Duke of Athens*

HIPPOLYTA, *Queen of the Amazons, betrothed to Theseus*

EGEUS, *an old man, father to Hermia*

LYSANDER ⎫ *young gentlemen, in love with*
DEMETRIUS ⎭ *Hermia*

PHILOSTRATE, *master of the revels to Theseus*

HERMIA (*short and dark*), *daughter to Egeus, in love with Lysander*

HELENA (*tall and fair*), *in love with Demetrius*

PETER QUINCE, *a carpenter*

NICK BOTTOM, *a weaver*

FRANCIS FLUTE, *a bellows-mender*

TOM SNOUT, *a tinker*

ROBIN STARVELING, *a tailor*

SNUG, *a joiner*

OBERON, *King of the Fairies*

TITANIA, *Queen of the Fairies*

ROBIN GOODFELLOW, THE PUCK

PEASEBLOSSOM ⎫
COBWEB   ⎪
MOTH   ⎬ *fairies*
MUSTARDSEED ⎭

Other fairies attending their King and Queen

Attendants on Theseus and Hippolyta

A MIDSUMMER-NIGHT'S DREAM

[1.1.] *The hall in the palace of Duke Theseus. On one
side a small platform with two chairs of state; on the
other side a hearth; at the back doors to right and left,
the wall between them opening out into a lobby*

*Theseus and Hippolyta enter and take their seats,
followed by Philostrate and attendants*

Theseus. Now, fair Hippolyta, our nuptial hour
Draws on apace: four happy days bring in
Another moon: but O, methinks how slow
This old moon wanes! she lingers my desires,
Like to a step-dame, or a dowager,
Long withering out a young man's revenue.
Hippolyta. Four days will quickly steep themselves
        in night:
Four nights will quickly dream away the time:
And then the moon, like to a silver bow
New-bent in heaven, shall behold the night   10
Of our solemnities.
Theseus.   Go, Philostrate,
Stir up the Athenian youth to merriments,
Awake the pert and nimble spirit of mirth,
Turn melancholy forth to funerals:
The pale companion is not for our pomp.
                    [*Philostrate bows and departs*
Hippolyta, I wooed thee with my sword,
And won thy love doing thee injuries:
But I will wed thee in another key,
With pomp, with triumph, and with revelling.

Egeus enters, haling along his daughter HERMIA *by the arm, followed by* LYSANDER *and* DEMETRIUS

20   *Egeus* [*bows*]. Happy be Theseus, our renownéd duke.
    Theseus. Thanks, good Egeus. What's the news
      with thee?
    Egeus. Full of vexation come I, with complaint
    Against my child, my daughter Hermia.
    Stand forth, Demetrius. My noble lord,
    This man hath my consent to marry her.
    Stand forth, Lysander. And, my gracious duke,
    This man hath witched the bosom of my child.
    Thou, thou, Lysander, thou hast given her rhymes,
    And interchanged love-tokens with my child:
30   Thou hast by moonlight at her window sung,
    With feigning voice, verses of feigning love:
    And stol'n the impression of her fantasy
    With bracelets of thy hair, rings, gauds, conceits,
    Knacks, trifles, nosegays, sweetmeats—messengers
    Of strong prevailment in unhardened youth.
    With cunning hast thou filched my daughter's heart,
    Turned her obedience, which is due to me,
    To stubborn harshness. And, my gracious duke,
    Be it so she will not here before your grace
40   Consent to marry with Demetrius,
    I beg the ancient privilege of Athens:
    As she is mine, I may dispose of her:
    Which shall be either to this gentleman,
    Or to her death; according to our law
    Immediately provided in that case.
      Theseus. What say you, Hermia? be advised,
        fair maid.
    To you your father should be as a god;
    One that composed your beauties; yea and one
    To whom you are but as a form in wax

By him imprinted, and within his power   50
To leave the figure or disfigure it.
Demetrius is a worthy gentleman.
 Hermia. So is Lysander.
 Theseus.   In himself he is:
But in this kind, wanting your father's voice,
The other must be held the worthier.
 Hermia. I would my father looked but with my eyes.
 Theseus. Rather your eyes must with his judge-
         ment look.
 Hermia. I do entreat your grace to pardon me.
I know not by what power I am made bold;
Nor how it may concern my modesty   60
In such a presence here to plead my thoughts:
But I beseech your grace that I may know
The worst that may befall me in this case
If I refuse to wed Demetrius.
 Theseus. Either to die the death, or to abjure
For ever the society of men.
Therefore, fair Hermia, question your desires,
Know of your youth, examine well your blood,
Whether, if you yield not to your father's choice,
You can endure the livery of a nun,   70
For aye to be in shady cloister mewed,
To live a barren sister all your life,
Chanting faint hymns to the cold fruitless moon.
Thrice blessèd they that master so their blood,
To undergo such maiden pilgrimage:
But earthlier happy is the rose distilled,
Than that which withering on the virgin thorn
Grows, lives and dies in single blessedness.
 Hermia. So will I grow, so live, so die, my lord,
Ere I will yield my virgin patent up   80
Unto his lordship, whose unwishèd yoke
My soul consents not to give sovereignty.

Theseus. Take time to pause, and by the next
    new moon—
The sealing-day betwixt my love and me
For everlasting bond of fellowship—
Upon that day either prepare to die
For disobedience to your father's will,
Or else to wed Demetrius as he would,
Or on Diana's altar to protest
90 For aye austerity and single life.
   Demetrius. Relent, sweet Hermia—and, Lysander, yield
Thy crazéd title to my certain right.
   Lysander. You have her father's love, Demetrius;
Let me have Hermia's: do you marry him.
   Egeus. Scornful Lysander! true, he hath my love;
And what is mine my love shall render him.
And she is mine, and all my right of her
I do estate unto Demetrius.
   Lysander. I am, my lord, as well derived as he,
100 As well possessed: my love is more than his:
My fortunes every way as fairly ranked—
If not with vantage—as Demetrius':
And, which is more than all these boasts can be,
I am beloved of beauteous Hermia.
Why should not I then prosecute my right?
Demetrius, I'll avouch it to his head,
Made love to Nedar's daughter, Helena,
And won her soul; and she, sweet lady, dotes,
Devoutly dotes, dotes in idolatry,
110 Upon this spotted and inconstant man.
   Theseus. I must confess that I have heard so much:
And with Demetrius thought to have spoke thereof;
But, being over-full of self-affairs,
My mind did lose it. [*he rises*] But Demetrius come,
And come Egeus, you shall go with me:
I have some private schooling for you both.

For you, fair Hermia, look you arm yourself
To fit your fancies to your father's will;
Or else the law of Athens yields you up
(Which by no means we may extenuate)   120
To death, or to a vow of single life.
Come, my Hippolyta: what cheer, my love?
Demetrius and Egeus, go along:
I must employ you in some business
Against our nuptial, and confer with you
Of something nearly that concerns yourselves.
    Egeus. With duty and desire we follow you.
                    [*all depart save Hermia and Lysander*
    Lysander. How now, my love? Why is your cheek
        so pale?
How chance the roses there do fade so fast?
    Hermia. Belike for want of rain, which I could well 130
Beteem them from the tempest of my eyes.
    Lysander. Ay me! [*he comforts her*] for aught that I
        could ever read,
Could ever hear by tale or history
The course of true love never did run smooth;
But, either it was different in blood—
    Hermia. O cross! too high to be enthralled to low.
    Lysander. Or else misgraffed in respect of years—
    Hermia. O spite! too old to be engaged to young.
    Lysander. Or else it stood upon the choice of friends—
    Hermia. O hell! to choose love by another's eyes!   140
    Lysander. Or, if there were a sympathy in choice,
War, death, or sickness did lay siege to it—
Making it momentany as a sound,
Swift as a shadow, short as any dream,
Brief as the lightning in the collied night
That, in a spleen, unfolds both heaven and earth;
And ere a man hath power to say 'Behold!'
The jaws of darkness do devour it up:

So quick bright things come to confusion.

150   *Hermia*. If then true lovers have been ever crossed,
It stands as an edict in destiny:
Then let us teach our trial patience,
Because it is a customary cross,
As due to love as thoughts and dreams and sighs,
Wishes and tears; poor Fancy's followers.

  Lysander. A good persuasion: therefore hear me,
    Hermia:
I have a widow aunt, a dowager
Of great revénue, and she hath no child:
From Athens is her house remote seven leagues:

160 And she respects me as her only son...
There, gentle Hermia, may I marry thee:
And to that place the sharp Athenian law
Cannot pursue us. If thou lovest me then,
Steal forth thy father's house to-morrow night;
And in the wood, a league without the town,
Where I did meet thee once with Helena,
To do observance to a morn of May,
There will I stay for thee.

  Hermia.   My good Lysander,
I swear to thee by Cupid's strongest bow,

170 By his best arrow with the golden head,
By the simplicity of Venus' doves,
By that which knitteth souls and prospers loves,
And by that fire which burned the Carthage queen,
When the false Troyan under sail was seen,
By all the vows that ever men have broke—
In number more than ever women spoke—
In that same place thou hast appointed me,
To-morrow truly will I meet with thee.

  Lysander. Keep promise, love...Look, here comes
    Helena.

Helena is seen passing through the lobby

Hermia. God speed, fair Helena: whither away? 180
Helena [*coming forward into the hall*]. Call you me
    fair? that 'fair' again unsay.
Demetrius loves your fair: O happy fair!
Your eyes are lode-stars, and your tongue's sweet air
More tuneable than lark to shepherd's ear,
When wheat is green, when hawthorn buds appear.
Sickness is catching: O, were favour so,
Yours would I catch, fair Hermia, ere I go!
My ear should catch your voice, my eye your eye,
My tongue should catch your tongue's sweet melody.
Were the world mine, Demetrius being bated, 190
The rest I'ld give to be to you translated.
O, teach me how you look, and with what art
You sway the motion of Demetrius' heart.
  Hermia. I frown upon him; yet he loves me still.
  Helena. O that your frowns would teach my smiles
    such skill.
  Hermia. I give him curses; yet he gives me love.
  Helena. O that my prayers could such affection move.
  Hermia. The more I hate, the more he follows me.
  Helena. The more I love, the more he hateth me.
  Hermia. His folly, Helena, is no fault of mine. 200
  Helena. None, but your beauty; would that fault
    were mine.
  Hermia. Take comfort: he no more shall see my face:
Lysander and myself will fly this place.
Before the time I did Lysander see,
Seemed Athens as a paradise to me:
O then, what graces in my love do dwell,
That he hath turned a heaven unto a hell!
  Lysander. Helen, to you our minds we will unfold:

To-morrow night, when Phœbe doth behold
210 Her silver visage in the wat'ry glass,
Decking with liquid pearl the bladed grass—
A time that lovers' flights doth still conceal—
Through Athens' gates have we devised to steal.
   Hermia. And in the wood, where often you and I
Upon faint primrose beds were wont to lie,
Emptying our bosoms of their counsel sweet,
There my Lysander and myself shall meet,
And thence from Athens turn away our eyes,
To seek new friends and stranger companies.
220 Farewell, sweet playfellow: pray thou for us:
And good luck grant thee thy Demetrius!
Keep word, Lysander: we must starve our sight
From lovers' food till morrow deep midnight. [*she goes*
   Lysander. I will, my Hermia. Helena, adieu:
As you on him, Demetrius dote on you!   [*he goes*
   Helena. How happy some o'er other some can be!
Through Athens I am thought as fair as she,
But what of that? Demetrius thinks not so:
He will not know what all but he do know.
230 And as he errs, doting on Hermia's eyes,
So I, admiring of his qualities.
Things base and vile, holding no quantity,
Love can transpose to form and dignity.
Love looks not with the eyes, but with the mind:
And therefore is winged Cupid painted blind.
Nor hath Love's mind of any judgement taste:
Wings and no eyes figure unheedy haste.
And therefore is Love said to be a child:
Because in choice he is so oft beguiled.
240 As waggish boys in game themselves forswear:
So the boy Love is perjured every where.
For ere Demetrius looked on Hermia's eyne,
He hailed down oaths that he was only mine.

And when this hail some heat from Hermia felt,
So he dissolved, and show'rs of oaths did melt.
I will go tell him of fair Hermia's flight:
Then to the wood will he to-morrow night
Pursue her: and for this intelligence
If I have thanks, it is a dear expense:
But herein mean I to enrich my pain,   250
To have his sight thither and back again.   [*she goes*

[1.2.]   *A room in the cottage of Peter Quince*

QUINCE, BOTTOM, SNUG, FLUTE, SNOUT, *and*
STARVELING

Quince. Is all our company here?

Bottom. You were best to call them generally, man by
man, according to the scrip.

Quince. Here is the scroll of every man's name, which
is thought fit, through all Athens, to play in our interlude
before the duke and the duchess, on his wedding-day at
night.

Bottom. First, good Peter Quince, say what the play
treats on: then read the names of the actors: and so
grow to a point.   10

Quince. Marry, our play is 'The most lamentable
comedy, and most cruel death of Pyramus and Thisby.'

Bottom. A very good piece of work, I assure you, and a
merry. Now, good Peter Quince, call forth your actors
by the scroll. Masters, spread yourselves.

Quince. Answer, as I call you. Nick Bottom, the weaver.

Bottom. Ready: name what part I am for, and proceed.

Quince. You, Nick Bottom, are set down for Pyramus.

Bottom. What is Pyramus? a lover, or a tyrant?

Quince. A lover that kills himself, most gallant for love. 20

Bottom. That will ask some tears in the true performing
of it. If I do it, let the audience look to their eyes:

I will move storms: I will condole in some measure.
To the rest—yet my chief humour is for a tyrant.
I could play Ercles rarely, or a part to tear a cat in, to
make all split.

> 'The raging rocks
> And shivering shocks
> Shall break the locks
> Of prison-gates,
> And Phibbus' car
> Shall shine from far
> And make and mar
> The foolish Fates.'

This was lofty. Now name the rest of the players. This
is Ercles' vein, a tyrant's vein: a lover is more condoling.

Quince. Francis Flute, the bellows-mender.

Flute. Here, Peter Quince.

Quince. Flute, you must take Thisby on you.

Flute. What is Thisby? a wand'ring knight?

Quince. It is the lady that Pyramus must love.

Flute. Nay, faith: let not me play a woman: I have a
beard coming.

Quince. That's all one: you shall play it in a mask: and
you may speak as small as you will.

Bottom. An I may hide my face, let me play Thisby too:
I'll speak in a monstrous little voice. 'Thisne? Thisne?'—
'Ah, Pyramus, my lover dear, thy Thisby dear, and
lady dear.'

Quince. No, no, you must play Pyramus: and Flute,
you Thisby.

Bottom. Well, proceed.

Quince. Robin Starveling, the tailor.

Starveling. Here, Peter Quince.

Quince. Robin Starveling, you must play Thisby's
mother. Tom Snout, the tinker.

Snout. Here, Peter Quince.

Quince. You, Pyramus' father, myself, Thisby's father; Snug, the joiner, you the lion's part: and I hope here is a play fitted.   60

Snug. Have you the lion's part written? pray you, if it be, give it me: for I am slow of study.

Quince. You may do it extempore: for it is nothing but roaring.

Bottom. Let me play the lion too. I will roar that I will do any man's heart good to hear me. I will roar that I will make the duke say, 'Let him roar again: let him roar again.'

Quince. An you should do it too terribly, you would fright the duchess and the ladies, that they would shriek: 70 and that were enough to hang us all.

All. That would hang us, every mother's son.

Bottom. I grant you, friends if you should fright the ladies out of their wits, they would have no more discretion but to hang us: but I will aggravate my voice so, that I will roar you as gently as any sucking dove: I will roar you an 'twere any nightingale

Quince. You can play no part but Pyramus: for Pyramus is a sweet-faced man; a proper man as one shall see in a summer's day; a most lovely, gentleman-like man: 80 therefore you must needs play Pyramus.

Bottom. Well, I will undertake it. What beard were I best to play it in?

Quince. Why, what you will.

Bottom. I will discharge it in either your straw-colour beard, your orange-tawny beard, your purple-in-grain beard, or your French-crown-colour beard, your perfect yellow.

Quince. Some of your French crowns have no hair at all; and then you will play barefaced....[*he distributes* 90 *strips of paper among them*] But, masters, here are your parts, and I am to entreat you, request you, and desire you, to con them by to-morrow night: and meet me in the palace wood, a mile without the town, by moonlight; there will we rehearse: for if we meet in the city, we shall be dogged with company, and our devices known. In the meantime, I will draw a bill of properties, such as our play wants. I pray you, fail me not.

Bottom. We will meet, and there we may rehease most obscenely and courageously. Take pains, be perfect: adieu.

100

Quince. At the duke's oak we meet.

Bottom. Enough: hold, or cut bow-strings.   [*they go*

[2.1.] *The palace wood, a league from Athens. A mossy stretch of broken ground, cleared of trees by wood-cutters and surrounded by thickets. Moonlight*

PUCK *and a* FAIRY, *meeting*

Puck. How now, spirit! whither wander you?

Fairy. Over hill, over dale,

    Thorough bush, thorough briar,

Over park, over pale,

    Thorough flood, thorough fire,

I do wander every where,

Swifter than the moonës sphere:

And I serve the Fairy Queen,

To dew her orbs upon the green.

10   The cowslips tall her pensioners be,

In their gold coats spots you see:

Those be rubies, fairy favours:

In those freckles live their savours.

I must go seek some dewdrops here,

And hang a pearl in every cowslip's ear.

Farewell, thou lob of spirits: I'll be gone——

Our queen and all her elves come here anon.

Puck. The king doth keep his revels here to-night.
Take heed the queen come not within his sight.
For Oberon is passing fell and wrath,   20
Because that she as her attendant hath
A lovely boy, stol'n from an Indian king:
She never had so sweet a changeling.
And jealous Oberon would have the child
Knight of his train, to trace the forests wild.
But she, perforce, withholds the lovéd boy,
Crowns him with flowers, and makes him all her joy.
And now they never meet in grove, or green,
By fountain clear, or spangled starlight sheen,
But they do square—that all their elves, for fear,   30
Creep into acorn cups and hide them there.
Fairy. Either I mistake your shape and making quite
Or else you are that shrewd and knavish sprite
Called Robin Goodfellow. Are not you he
That frights the maidens of the villagery,
Skim milk, and sometimes labour in the quern,
And bootless make the breathless housewife churn,
And sometime make the drink to bear no barm,
Mislead night-wanderers, laughing at their harm?
Those that Hobgoblin call you and sweet Puck,   40
You do their work, and they shall have good luck.
Are not you he?
Puck.   Thou speak'st aright;
I am that merry wanderer of the night.
I jest to Oberon, and make him smile
When I a fat and bean-fed horse beguile,
Neighing in likeness of a filly foal;
And sometime lurk I in a gossip's bowl,
In very likeness of a roasted crab,
And, when she drinks, against her lips I bob,
And on her withered dewlap pour the ale.   50

The wisest aunt, telling the saddest tale,
Sometime for three-foot stool mistaketh me:
Then slip I from her bum, down topples she,
And 'tailor' cries, and falls into a cough:
And then the whole choir hold their hips and laugh,
And waxen in their mirth, and neeze, and swear
A merrier hour was never wasted there.
But room, faëry: here comes Oberon.

Fairy. And here my mistress. Would that he were gone.

*The clearing is suddenly thronged with fairies:
OBERON and TITANIA confront each other*

50   *Oberon.* Ill met by moonlight, proud Titania.
Titania. What, jealous Oberon! Fairies, skip hence—
I have forsworn his bed and company.
Oberon. Tarry, rash wanton. Am not I thy lord?
Titania. Then I must be thy lady: but I know
When thou hast stol'n away from fairy land,
And in the shape of Corin sat all day,
Playing on pipes of corn, and versing love,
To amorous Phillida. Why art thou here,
Come from the farthest steep of India?

70   But that, forsooth, the bouncing Amazon,
Your buskined mistress and your warrior love,
To Theseus must be wedded; and you come
To give their bed joy and prosperity.
Oberon. How canst thou thus for shame, Titania,
Glance at my credit with Hippolyta,
Knowing I know thy love to Theseus?
Didst thou not lead him through the glimmering night
From Perigouna, whom he ravishéd?
And make him with fair Ægles break his faith,

80   With Ariadne, and Antiopa?
Titania. These are the forgeries of jealousy:

And never, since the middle summer's spring,
Met we on hill, in dale, forest, or mead,
By pavéd fountain, or by rushy brook,
Or in the beachéd margent of the sea,
To dance our ringlets to the whistling wind,
But with thy brawls thou hast disturbed our sport.
Therefore the winds, piping to us in vain,
As in revenge, have sucked up from the sea
Contagious fogs: which falling in the land,   90
Hath every pelting river made so proud
That they have overborne their continents.
The ox hath therefore stretched his yoke in vain,
The ploughman lost his sweat, and the green corn
Hath rotted ere his youth attained a beard;
The fold stands empty in the drownéd field,
And crows are fatted with the murrion flock;
The nine men's morris is filled up with mud,
And the quaint mazes in the wanton green
For lack of tread are indistinguishable.   100
†The human mortals want their winter cheer;
No night is now with hymn or carol blest;
Therefore the moon, the governess of floods,
Pale in her anger, washes all the air,
That rheumatic diseases do abound.
And thorough this distemperature we see
The seasons alter: hoary-headed frosts
Fall in the fresh lap of the crimson rose,
And on old Hiems' thin and icy crown
An odorous chaplet of sweet summer buds   110
Is, as in mockery, set. The spring, the summer,
The childing autumn, angry winter, change
Their wonted liveries; and the mazéd world,
By their increase, now knows not which is which.
And this same progeny of evils comes

From our debate, from our dissension:
We are their parents and original.
  Oberon. Do you amend it then: it lies in you.
Why should Titania cross her Oberon?
120 I do but beg a little changeling boy,
To be my henchman.
  Titania.   Set your heart at rest,
The fairy land buys not the child of me.
His mother was a vot'ress of my order;
And in the spicéd Indian air, by night,
Full often hath she gossiped by my side;
And sat with me on Neptune's yellow sands,
Marking th'embarkéd traders on the flood;
When we have laughed to see the sails conceive
And grow big-bellied with the wanton wind;
130 Which she, with pretty and with swimming gait
Following—her womb then rich with my young squire—
Would imitate, and sail upon the land,
To fetch me trifles, and return again,
As from a voyage, rich with merchandise.
But she, being mortal, of that boy did die;
And for her sake do I rear up her boy;
And for her sake I will not part with him.
Oberon. How long within this wood intend you stay?
Titania. Perchance till after Theseus' wedding-day.
140 If you will patiently dance in our round,
And see our moonlight revels, go with us:
If not, shun me, and I will spare your haunts.
  Oberon. Give me that boy, and I will go with thee.
  Titania. Not for thy fairy kingdom....Fairies, away!
We shall chide downright, if I longer stay.
                [Titania departs in anger with her train
  Oberon. Well: go thy way. Thou shalt not from
    this grove,
Till I torment thee for this injury.

My gentle Puck, come hither. Thou rememb'rest
Since once I sat upon a promontory,
And heard a mermaid, on a dolphin's back,   150
Uttering such dulcet and harmonious breath
That the rude sea grew civil at her song,
And certain stars shot madly from their spheres
To hear the sea-maid's music.

   Puck.   I remember.

   Oberon. That very time I saw—but thou couldst not—
Flying between the cold moon and the earth,
Cupid all armed: a certain aim he took
At a fair Vestal, thronéd by the west,
And loosed his love-shaft smartly from his bow,
As it should pierce a hundred thousand hearts: 160
But I might see young Cupid's fiery shaft
Quenched in the chaste beams of the wat'ry moon:
And the imperial Vot'ress passéd on,
In maiden meditation, fancy-free.
Yet marked I where the bolt of Cupid fell.
It fell upon a little western flower;
Before, milk-white; now purple with love's wound—
And maidens call it Love-in-idleness.
Fetch me that flower, the herb I showed thee once.
The juice of it, on sleeping eyelids laid,   170
Will make or man or woman madly dote
Upon the next live creature that it sees.
Fetch me this herb, and be thou here again
Ere the leviathan can swim a league.

   Puck. I'll put a girdle round about the earth
In forty minutes.   [*he vanishes*

   Oberon.   Having once this juice,
I'll watch Titania when she is asleep,
And drop the liquor of it in her eyes:
The next thing then she waking looks upon—
Be it on lion, bear, or wolf, or bull,   180

On meddling monkey, or on busy ape—
She shall pursue it with the soul of love.
And ere I take this charm from off her sight—
As I can take it with another herb—
I'll make her render up her page to me.
But who comes here? I am invisible,
And I will overhear their conference.

DEMETRIUS enters the clearing, 'HELENA following him'

   Demetrius. I love thee not...therefore pursue me not.
Where is Lysander and fair Hermia?
190 The one I'll slay...the other slayeth me.
Thou told'st me they were stol'n unto this wood:
And here am I, and wood within this wood,
Because I cannot meet my Hermia:
Hence, get thee gone, and follow me no more.
   Helena. You draw me, you hard-hearted adamant;
But yet you draw not iron, for my heart
Is true as steel. Leave you your power to draw,
And I shall have no power to follow you.
   Demetrius. Do I entice you? Do I speak you fair
200 Or rather do I not in plainest truth
Tell you I do not nor I cannot love you?
   Helena. And even for that do I love you the more:
I am your spaniel; and, Demetrius,
The more you beat me, I will fawn on you.
Use me but as your spaniel: spurn me, strike me,
Neglect me, lose me: only give me leave,
Unworthy as I am, to follow you.
What worser place can I beg in your love.—
And yet a place of high respect with me—
210 Than to be uséd as you use your dog?
   Demetrius. Tempt not too much the hatred of
     my spirit,
For I am sick when I do look on thee.

Helena. And I am sick when I look not on you.
  Demetrius. You do impeach your modesty too much
To leave the city and commit yourself
Into the hands of one that loves you not,
To trust the opportunity of night
And the ill counsel of a desert place
With the rich worth of your virginity.
  Helena. Your virtue is my privilege for that: 220
It is not night when I do see your face,
Therefore I think I am not in the night—
Nor doth this wood lack worlds of company,
For you in my respect are all the world.
Then how can it be said I am alone
When all the world is here to look on me?
  Demetrius. I'll run from thee and hide me in the brakes,
And leave thee to the mercy of wild beasts.
  Helena. The wildest hath not such a heart as you.
Run when you will; the story shall be changed: 230
Apollo flies, and Daphne holds the chase;
The dove pursues the griffin; the mild hind
Makes speed to catch the tiger....bootless speed,
When cowardice pursues and valour flies.
  Demetrius. I will not stay thy questions—let me go:
Or, if thou follow me, do not believe
But I shall do thee mischief in the wood.
  Helena. Ay, in the temple, in the town, the field,
You do me mischief. Fie, Demetrius!
Your wrongs do set a scandal on my sex: 240
We cannot fight for love, as men may do;
We should be wooed and were not made to woo   [*he goes*]
I'll follow thee and make a heaven of hell,
To die upon the hand I love so well. [*she follows after*
  Oberon. Fare thee well, nymph. Ere he do leave
    this grove,
Thou shalt fly him, and he shall seek thy love.

PUCK reappears

Welcome, wanderer. Hast thou the flower there?
  Puck. Ay, there it is.
  Oberon.   I pray thee, give it me.
I know a bank where the wild thyme blows,
250 Where oxlips and the nodding violet grows,
Quite over-canopied with luscious woodbine,
With sweet musk-roses, and with eglantine:
There sleeps Titania sometime of the night,
Lulled in these flowers with dances and delight;
And there the snake throws her enamelled skin,
Weed wide enough to wrap a fairy in.
And with the juice of this I'll streak her eyes,
And make her full of hateful fantasies.
Take thou some of it, and seek through this grove:
260 A sweet Athenian lady is in love
With a disdainful youth; anoint his eyes—
But do it when the next thing he espies
May be the lady. Thou shalt know the man
By the Athenian garments he hath on.
Effect it with some care, that he may prove
More fond on her than she upon her love.
And look thou meet me ere the first cock crow.
  Puck. Fear not, my lord: your servant shall do so.
                               [*they depart*

[2.2.] *Another part of the wood. A grassy plot before a great oak-tree; behind the tree a high bank overhung with creepers, and at one side a thorn-bush. The air is heavy with the scent of blossom*

    TITANIA lies couched in her bower beneath the bank; her fairies attending her

  Titania. Come now, a roundel and a fairy song:
Then, for the third part of a minute, hence—
Some to kill cankers in the musk-rose buds,

Some war with rere-mice for their leathern wings,
To make my small elves coats, and some keep back
The clamorous owl that nightly hoots and wonders
At our quaint spirits. Sing me now asleep;
Then to your offices, and let me rest.

'Fairies sing'

You spotted snakes, with double tongue,
   Thorny hedgehogs, be not seen;   10
Newts and blind-worms do no wrong,
   Come not near our Fairy Queen.

Philomele, with melody,
Sing in our sweet lullaby,
   Lulla, lulla, lullaby,
   Lulla, lulla, lullaby,
  Never harm,
  Nor spell, nor charm,
Come our lovely lady nigh.
So good night, with lullaby.   20

1 Fairy. Weaving spiders come not here:
   Hence you long-legged spinners, hence:
Beetles black approach not near:
   Worm nor snail do no offence.

Philomele, with melody,
Sing in our sweet lullaby,
   Lulla, lulla, lullaby,
   Lulla, lulla, lullaby,
  Never harm,
  Nor spell, nor charm,   30
Come our lovely lady nigh.
So good night, with lullaby.   [*Titania sleeps*

2 Fairy. Hence, away: now all is well:
   One aloof stand sentinel.
               [*the fairies steal away*

Oberon appears, hovering above the bank; he alights and
anoints the eyes of Titania with the juice of the flower

Oberon. What thou see'st when thou dost wake,
Do it for thy true-love take;
Love and languish for his sake.
Be it ounce, or cat, or bear,
Pard, or boar with bristled hair,
40 In thy eye that shall appear
When thou wak'st, it is thy dear:
Wake when some vile thing is near.   [*he vanishes*

Lysander approaches with Hermia leaning upon his arm

Lysander. Fair love, you faint with wand'ring in
      the wood;
    And to speak troth I have forgot our way.
We'll rest us, Hermia, if you think it good,
    And tarry for the comfort of the day.
Hermia. Be't so, Lysander: find you out a bed:
For I upon this bank will rest my head.
Lysander. One turf shall serve as pillow for us both,
50 One heart, one bed, two bosoms, and one troth.
Hermia. Nay, good Lysander: for my sake, my dear,
Lie further off yet; do not lie so near.
Lysander. O take the sense, sweet, of my innocence!
Love takes the meaning in love's conference.
I mean that my heart unto yours is knit,
So that but one heart we can make of it:
Two bosoms interchainéd with an oath,
So then two bosoms and a single troth.
Then by your side no bed-room me deny,
60 For lying so, Hermia, I do not lie.
Hermia. Lysander riddles very prettily.
Now much beshrew my manners and my pride,
If Hermia meant to say Lysander lied.
But, gentle friend, for love and courtesy

Lie further off—in human modesty:
Such separation as may well be said
Becomes a virtuous bachelor and a maid,
So far be distant—and good night, sweet friend:
Thy love ne'er alter till thy sweet life end!

   Lysander. Amen, amen, to that fair prayer, say I—   70
And then end life when I end loyalty!
Here is my bed: sleep give thee all his rest.

   Hermia. With half that wish the wisher's eyes
      be pressed.   *PUCK appears*   ['*they sleep*'

Puck. Through the forest have I gone,
      But Athenian found I none
      On whose eyes I might approve
      This flower's force in stirring love.
      Night and silence—who is here?
      Weeds of Athens he doth wear:
      This is he, my master said,   80
      Despiséd the Athenian maid:
      And here the maiden, sleeping sound,
      On the dank and dirty ground.
      Pretty soul, she durst not lie
      Near this lack-love, this kill-courtesy.
           [*he anoints the eyelids of Lysander*
      Churl, upon thy eyes I throw
      All the power this charm doth owe:
      When thou wak'st, let love forbid
      Sleep his seat on thy eyelid.
      So awake when I am gone;   90
      For I must now to Oberon.   [*he vanishes*

'*Enter DEMETRIUS and HELENA, running*'

Helena. Stay; though thou kill me, sweet Demetrius.
Demetrius. I charge thee, hence, and do not haunt
   me thus.

Helena. O, wilt thou darkling leave me? do not so.
Demetrius. Stay, on thy peril; I alone will go.
   [*he breaks from her and disappears into the wood*
Helena. O, I am out of breath in this fond chase!
The more my prayer, the lesser is my grace.
Happy is Hermia, wheresoe'er she lies;
For she hath blessèd and attractive eyes.
100 How came her eyes so bright? Not with salt tears—
If so, my eyes are oft'ner washed than hers.
No, no: I am as ugly as a bear,
For beasts that meet me run away for fear.
Therefore no marvel though Demetrius
Do, as a monster, fly my presence thus.
What wicked and dissembling glass of mine
Made me compare with Hermia's sphery eyne?
But who is here? Lysander! on the ground!
Dead? or asleep? I see no blood, no wound.
110 Lysander, if you live, good sir, awake.
 Lysander [leaps up]. And run through fire I will, for
  thy sweet sake.
Transparent Helena! Nature shows her art,
That through thy bosom makes me see thy heart.
Where is Demetrius? O, how fit a word
Is that vile name to perish on my sword!
 Helena. Do not say so, Lysander, say not so.
What though he love your Hermia? Lord! what though?
Yet Hermia still loves you: then be content.
 Lysander. Content with Hermia? No: I do repent
120 The tedious minutes I with her have spent.
Not Hermia, but Helena I love—
Who will not change a raven for a dove?
The will of man is by his reason swayed;
And reason says you are the worthier maid.
Things growing are not ripe until their season:
So I, being young, till now ripe not to reason—

And touching now the point of human skill,
Reason becomes the marshal to my will,
And leads me to your eyes; where I o'erlook
Love's stories, written in Love's richest book.   130
  Helena. Wherefore was I to this keen mockery born?
When at your hands did I deserve this scorn?
Is't not enough, is't not enough, young man,
That I did never, no, nor never can,
Deserve a sweet look from Demetrius' eye,
But you must flout my insufficiency?
Good troth, you do me wrong, good sooth, you do,
In such disdainful manner me to woo.
But fare you well: perforce I must confess
I thought you lord of more true gentleness.   140
O, that a lady, of one man refused,
Should of another therefore be abused!   [*she goes*
  Lysander. She sees not Hermia. Hermia, sleep
    thou there,
And never mayst thou come Lysander near.
For, as a surfeit of the sweetest things
The deepest loathing to the stomach brings,
Or as the heresies that men do leave
Are hated most of those they did deceive,
So thou, my surfeit and my heresy,
Of all be hated, but the most of me!   150
And all my powers, address your love and might
To honour Helen, and to be her knight.
                   [*he follows Helena*
  Hermia [*awaking*]. Help me, Lysander, help me; do
    thy best
To pluck this crawling serpent from my breast.
Ay me, for pity! what a dream was here?
Lysander, look how I do quake with fear.
Methought a serpent eat my heart away,
And you sat smiling at his cruel prey....

Lysander! what, removed?—Lysander! lord!
160 What, out of hearing gone? no sound, no word?
Alack, where are you? speak, an if you hear;
Speak, of all loves! I swoon almost with fear.
No? then I will perceive you are not nigh.
Either dèath or you I'll find immediately.   [*she goes*

[3.1.] QUINCE (*carrying a bag*), SNUG, BOTTOM,
FLUTE, SNOUT, *and* STARVELING *come up severally or
in pairs and gather beneath the oak-tree*

Bottom. Are we all met?

Quince. Pat, pat: and here's a marvellous convenient
place for our rehearsal. This green plot shall be our
stage, this hawthorn-brake our tiring-house—and we
will do it in action as we will do it before the duke.

Bottom. Peter Quince!

Quince. What say'st thou, bully Bottom?

Bottom. There are things in this comedy of Pyramus
and Thisby that will never please. First, Pyramus must
10 draw a sword to kill himself; which the ladies cannot
abide. How answer you that?

Snout. By'r lakin, a parlous fear.

Starveling. I believe we must leave the killing out,
when all is done.

Bottom. Not a whit: I have a device to make all well.
Write me a prologue, and let the prologue seem to say
we will do no harm with our swords, and that Pyramus
is not killed indeed: and, for the more better assurance,
tell them that I, Pyramus, am not Pyramus but Bottom
20 the weaver: this will put them out of fear.

Quince. Well, we will have such a prologue, and it
shall be written in eight and six.

Bottom. No, make it two more: let it be written in
eight and eight.

Snout. Will not the ladies be afeard of the lion?

Starveling. I fear it, I promise you.

Bottom. Masters, you ought to consider with yourselves —to bring in (God shield us!) a lion among ladies is a most dreadful thing. For there is not a more fearful wild-fowl than your lion living; and we ought to look to't. 30

Snout. Therefore, another prologue must tell he is not a lion.

Bottom. Nay, you must name his name, and half his face must be seen through the lion's neck, and he himself must speak through, saying thus, or to the same defect: 'Ladies,' or 'Fair ladies—I would wish you,' or 'I would request you,' or 'I would entreat you, not to fear, not to tremble: my life for yours. If you think I come hither as a lion, it were pity of my life. No: I am no such thing: I am a man as other men are'. And there indeed 40 let him name his name, and tell them plainly he is Snug the joiner.

Quince. Well, it shall be so. But there is two hard things: that is, to bring the moonlight into a chamber: for you know, Pyramus and Thisby meet by moonlight.

Snout. Doth the moon shine that night we play our play?

Bottom. A calendar, a calendar! Look in the almanac; find out moonshine, find out moonshine.

Quince takes an almanac from his bag and searches therein

Quince. Yes, it doth shine that night. 50

Bottom. Why, then may you leave a casement of the great chamber window, where we play, open; and the moon may shine in at the casement.

Quince. Ay, or else one must come in with a bush of thorns and a lantern, and say he comes to disfigure or to present the person of Moonshine. Then, there is another thing: we must have a wall in the great chamber; for Pyramus and Thisby, says the story, did talk through the chink of a wall.

60 *Snout.* You can never bring in a wall. What say you, Bottom?

Bottom. Some man or other must present wall; and let him have some plaster, or some loam, or some rough-cast about him, to signify wall; and let him hold his fingers thus...[*he stretches out his fingers*] and through that cranny shall Pyramus and Thisby whisper.

Quince. If that may be, then all is well....[*takes out a book and opens it*] Come, sit down, every mother's son, and rehearse your parts. Pyramus, you begin: when

70 you have spoken your speech, enter into that brake—and so every one according to his cue.

PUCK *appears behind the oak*

(*Puck.* What hempen home-spuns have we swagg'ring here,
So near the cradle of the Fairy Queen?
What, a play toward? I'll be an auditor,
An actor too perhaps, if I see cause.
Quince. Speak, Pyramus. Thisby, stand forth.
Bottom. 'Thisby, the flowers ha' odious savours sweet,'—
Quince [*prompts*]. 'Odious'—odorous!
Bottom. —'odours savours sweet,

80 So hath thy breath, my dearest Thisby dear.
But hark, a voice! stay thou but here awhile,
And by and by I will to thee appear.'
[*exit into the brake*

(*Puck.* A stranger Pyramus than e'er played here!
[*he follows Bottom*

Flute. Must I speak now?

Quince. Ay, marry, must you. For you must understand he goes but to see a noise that he heard, and is to
come again.

Flute. 'Most radiant Pyramus, most lily-white of hue,
    Of colour like the red rose on triumphant briar,
Most brisky juvenal, and eke most lovely Jew,   90
    As true as truest horse that yet would never tire,
I'll meet thee, Pyramus, at Ninny's tomb.'

Quince. 'Ninus' tomb,' man! Why, you must not speak
that yet! That you answer to Pyramus. You speak all
your part at once, cues and all. Pyramus enter; your
cue is past; it is, 'never tire.'

Flute. O,—'As true as truest horse that yet would
    never tire.'

> *Enter from the brake* BOTTOM *with an ass's head;*
> PUCK *following*

Bottom. 'If I were fair, Thisby, I were only thine.'

Quince. O monstrous! O strange! We are haunted.
Pray, masters! fly, masters! help!   100

> [*they all run away and hide them in the bushes*

Puck. I'll follow you: I'll lead you about a round,
    Through bog, through bush, through brake,
        through briar;
Sometime a horse I'll be, sometime a hound,
    A hog, a headless bear, sometime a fire,
And neigh, and bark, and grunt, and roar, and burn,
Like horse, hound, hog, bear, fire, at every turn.

> [*he pursues them*

Bottom. Why do they run away? This is a knavery of
them to make me afeard.

> SNOUT *peers from behind a bush*

Snout. O Bottom, thou art changed! What do I see
on thee?   110

Bottom. What do you see? you see an ass-head of your own, do you? [*Snout disappears*

QUINCE *stealthily returns*

Quince. Bless thee Bottom, bless thee! thou art translated. [*he turns and flees*

Bottom. I see their knavery. This is to make an ass of me, to fright me if they could: but I will not stir from this place, do what they can. I will walk up and down here, and will sing that they shall hear I am not afraid....

[*he sings through his nose, braying at whiles*

The ousel cock, so black of hue,
With orange-tawny bill,
The throstle with his note so true,
The wren with little quill....

Titania [*comes from the bower*]. What angel wakes me from my flow'ry bed?

Bottom. The finch, the sparrow, and the lark,
The plain-song cuckoo gray:
Whose note full many a man doth mark,
And dares not answer, nay....

for indeed, who would set his wit to so foolish a bird? who would give a bird the lie, though he cry 'cuckoo' never so?

Titania. I pray thee, gentle mortal, sing again!
Mine ear is much enamoured of thy note;
So is mine eye enthrallèd to thy shape,
And thy fair virtue's force—perforce—doth move me,
On the first view, to say, to swear, I love thee.

Bottom. Methinks, mistress, you should have little reason for that. And yet, to say the truth, reason and love keep little company together now-a-days. The more the pity, that some honest neighbours will not make them friends. Nay, I can gleek upon occasion.

Titania. Thou art as wise as thou art beautiful.

Bottom. Not so, neither: but if I had wit enough to get
out of this wood, I have enough to serve mine owe turn.

Titania. Out of this wood do not desire to go:
Thou shalt remain here, whether thou wilt or no.
I am a spirit of no common rate:
The summer still doth tend upon my state,
And I do love thee: therefore go with me.
I'll give thee fairies to attend on thee:
And they shall fetch thee jewels from the deep,
And sing, while thou on presséd flowers dost sleep: 150
And I will purge thy mortal grossness so,
That thou shalt like an airy spirit go.   [*she calls*
Peaseblossom, Cobweb, Moth, and Mustardseed!

[*as she utters each name a fairy
alights before her and replies*

Peaseblossom. Ready!
Cobweb.   And I—
Moth.   And I—
Mustardseed.   And I—
All [*bowing*].   Where shall we go?

Titania. Be kind and courteous to this gentleman;
Hop in his walks and gambol in his eyes;
Feed him with apricocks and dewberries,
With purple grapes, green figs, and mulberries;
The honey-bags steal from the humble-bees,
And for night-tapers crop their waxen thighs,   160
And light them at the fiery glow-worm's eyes,
To have my love to bed and to arise;
And pluck the wings from painted butterflies,
To fan the moonbeams from his sleeping eyes.
Nod to him, elves, and do him courtesies.

Peaseblossom. Hail, mortal!
Cobweb. Hail!
Moth. Hail!

Mustardseed. Hail!

170 *Bottom.* I cry your worships mercy, heartily. I beseech your worship's name.

Cobweb [*bows*]. Cobweb.

Bottom. I shall desire you of more acquaintance, good Master Cobweb: if I cut my finger, I shall make bold with you. Your name, honest gentleman?

Peaseblosom [*bows*]. Peaseblossom.

Bottom. I pray you, commend me to Mistress Squash, your mother, and to Master Peascod, your father. Good Master Peaseblossom, I shall desire you of more

180 acquaintance too. Your name, I beseech you sir?

Mustardseed [*bows*]. Mustardseed.

Bottom. Good Master Mustardseed, I know your patience well. That same cowardly, giant-like, Oxbeef hath devoured many a gentleman of your house. I promise you your kindred hath made my eyes water ere now. I desire you of more acquaintance, good Master Mustardseed.

Titania. Come, wait upon him; lead him to my bower.
The moon, methinks, looks with a wat'ry eye:

190 And when she weeps, weeps every little flower,
    Lamenting some enforcéd chastity.
    Tie up my love's tongue, bring him silently.

                   [*they move towards the bower*

[3.2.]   *The clearing with the mossy slopes*

            OBERON *appears*

Oberon. I wonder if Titania be awaked;
Then, what it was that next came in her eye,
Which she must dote on in extremity.

         PUCK *enters the clearing*

Here comes my messenger. How now, mad spirit?

What night-rule now about this haunted grove?
  Puck. My mistress with a monster is in love.
Near to her close and consecrated bower,
While she was in her dull and sleeping hour,
A crew of patches, rude mechanicals
That work for bread upon Athenian stalls,   10
Were met together to rehearse a play
Intended for great Theseus' nuptial-day.
The shallowest thick-skin of that barren sort,
Who Pyramus presented, in their sport
Forsook his scene and ent'red in a brake;
When I did him at this advantage take,
An ass's noll I fixéd on his head.
Anon his Thisbe must be answeréd,
And forth my mimic comes. When they him spy,
As wild geese that the creeping fowler eye,   20
Or russet-pated choughs, many in sort,
Rising and cawing at the gun's report,
Sever themselves and madly sweep the sky,
So, at his sight, away his fellows fly;
†And at a stump here o'er and o'er one falls—
He 'murder' cries, and help from Athens calls.
Their sense thus weak, lost with their fears thus strong,
Made senseless things begin to do them wrong.
For briars and thorns at their apparel snatch:
Some sleeves, some hats; from yielders all things catch. 30
I led them on in this distracted fear,
And left sweet Pyramus translated there:
When in that moment (so it came to pass)
Titania waked and straightway loved an ass.
  Oberon. This falls out better than I could devise.
But hast thou yet latched the Athenian's eyes
With the love-juice, as I did bid thee do?
  Puck. I took him sleeping—that is finished too—

And the Athenian woman by his side;
40 That, when he waked, of fórce she must be eyed.

DEMETRIUS and HERMIA approach

Oberon. Stand close; this is the same Athenian.
Puck. This is the woman: but not this the man.
Demetrius. O, why rebuke you him that loves you so?
Lay breath so bitter on your bitter foe.
Hermia. Now I but chide: but I should use thee worse,
For thou, I fear, hast given me cause to curse...
If thou hast slain Lysander in his sleep,
Being o'er-shoes in blood, plunge in the deep,
And kill me too.
50 The sun was not so true unto the day
As he to me. Would he have stolen away
From sleeping Hermia? I'll believe as soon
This whole earth may be bored, and that the moon
May through the centre creep and so displease
Her brother's noontide with th'Antipodes.
It cannot be but thou hast murd'red him—
So should a murderer look; so dead, so grim.
Demetrius. So should the murdered look, and so
      should I,
Pierced through the heart with your stern cruelty.
60 Yet you, the murderer, look as bright, as clear,
As yonder Venus in her glimmering sphere.
Hermia. What's this to my Lysander? Where is he?
Ah, good Demetrius, wilt thou give him me?
Demetrius. I had rather give his carcase to my hounds.
Hermia. Out, dog! out, cur! thou driv'st me past
      the bounds
Of maiden's patience. Hast thou slain him then?
Henceforth be never numb'red among men!
O, once tell true: tell true, even for my sake:
Durst thou have looked upon him being awake?

And hast thou killed him, sleeping? O brave touch!   70
Could not a worm, an adder, do so much?
An adder did it; for with doubler tongue
Than thine, thou serpent, never adder stung.
  Demetrius. You spend your passion on a mis-
    prized mood:
I am not guilty of Lysander's blood;
Nor is he dead, for aught that I can tell.
  Hermia. I pray thee, tell me then that he is well.
  Demetrius. An if I could, what should I get therefore?
  Hermia. A privilege never to see me more,
And from thy hated presence part I so: 80
See me no more, whether he be dead or no.
                           [*she hurries away*
  Demetrius. There is no following her in this fierce vein.
Here therefore for a while I will remain.
So sorrow's heaviness doth heavier grow
For debt that bankrupt sleep doth sorrow owe;
Which now in some slight measure it will pay,
If for his tender here I make some stay.   [*he lies down*
  Oberon. What hast thou done? thou hast mis-
    taken quite,
And laid the love-juice on some true-love's sight.
Of thy misprision must perforce ensue   90
Some true love turned, and not a false turned true.
  Puck. Then fate o'er-rules, that, one man holding troth.
A million fail, confounding oath on oath.
  Oberon. About the wood go swifter than the wind,
And Helena of Athens look thou find.
All fancy-sick she is, and pale of cheer
With sighs of love that costs the fresh blood dear.
By some illusion see thou bring her here:
I'll charm his eyes against she do appear.
  Puck. I go, I go—look how I go—   100
Swifter than arrow from the Tartar's bow. [*he vanishes*

Oberon bends over the sleeping Demetrius

Oberon. Flower of this purple dye,
Hit with Cupid's archery,
Sink in apple of his eye.
When his love he doth espy,
Let her shine as gloriously
As the Venus of the sky.
When thou wak'st, if she be by,
Beg of her for remedy.

PUCK reappears

110   *Puck.* Captain of our fairy band,
Helena is here at hand,
And the youth, mistook by me,
Pleading for a lover's fee.
Shall we their fond pageant see?
Lord, what fools these mortals be!
    Oberon. Stand aside. The noise they make
Will cause Demetrius to awake.
    Puck. Then will two at once woo one;
That must needs be sport alone.
120   And those things do best please me
That befall prepost'rously. [*they stand aside*

HELENA comes up, followed by LYSANDER

Lysander. Why should you think that I should woo
  in scorn?
Scorn and derision never come in tears.
Look when I vow, I weep; and vows so born
  In their nativity all truth appears.
How can these things in me seem scorn to you,
Bearing the badge of faith to prove them true?
    Helena. You do advance your cunning more and more.
  When truth kills truth, O devilish-holy fray!

These vows are Hermia's—will you give her o'er?   130
   Weigh oath with oath, and you will nothing weigh:
Your vows, to her and me, put in two scales,
Will even weigh; and both as light as tales.

Lysander. I had no judgement when to her I swore.

Helena. Nor none, in my mind, now you give
    her o'er.

Lysander. Demetrius loves her: and he loves not you.

Demetrius [awaking]. O Helen, goddess, nymph,
    perfect, divine!
To what, my love, shall I compare thine eyne?
Crystal is muddy. O, how ripe in show
Thy lips, those kissing cherries, tempting grow!   140
That pure congealéd white, high Taurus' snow,
Fanned with the eastern wind, turns to a crow,
When thou hold'st up thy hand. O let me kiss
This princess of pure white, this seal of bliss!

Helena. O spite! O hell! I see you all are bent
To set against me for your merriment.
If you were civil and knew courtesy,
You would not do me thus much injury.
Can you not hate me, as I know you do,
But you must join in souls to mock me too?   150
If you were men, as men you are in show,
You would not use a gentle lady so:
To vow, and swear, and superpraise my parts,
When I am sure you hate me with your hearts.
You both are rivals, and love Hermia;
And now both rivals, to mock Helena.
A trim exploit, a manly enterprise,
To conjure tears up in a poor maid's eyes
With your derision! none of noble sort
Would so offend a virgin, and extort   160
A poor soul's patience, all to make you sport.

Lysander. You are unkind, Demetrius; be not so—
For you love Hermia; this you know I know;
And here, with all good will, with all my heart,
In Hermia's love I yield you up my part:
And yours of Helena to me bequeath,
Whom I do love, and will do till my death.

Helena. Never did mockers waste more idle breath.

Demetrius. Lysander, keep thy Hermia: I will none.
170 If e'er I loved her, all that love is gone.
My heart to her but as guest-wise sojourned,
And now to Helen is it home returned,
There to remain.

Lysander. Helen, it is not so.

Demetrius. Disparage not the faith thou dost not know,
Lest to thy peril thou aby it dear....

HERMIA is seen approaching

Look where thy love comes: yonder is thy dear.

HERMIA spies Lysander and runs towards him

Hermia. Dark night, that from the eye his
　　　　function takes,
The ear more quick of apprehension makes.
Wherein it doth impair the seeing sense,
180 It pays the hearing double recompense.
Thou art not by mine eye, Lysander, found;
Mine ear, I thank it, brought me to thy sound.
But why unkindly didst thou leave me so?

Lysander [*turning away*]. Why should he stay
　　　　whom love doth press to go?

Hermia. What love could press Lysander from
　　　　my side?

Lysander. Lysander's love, that would not let him bide—
Fair Helena! who more engilds the night
Than all yon fiery oes and eyes of light.

Why seek'st thou me? could not this make thee know
The hate I bear thee made me leave thee so?   190
  Hermia. You speak not as you think: it cannot be.
  Helena. Lo! she is one of this confederacy.
Now I perceive they have conjoined all three
To fashion this false sport in spite of me.
Injurious Hermia, most ungrateful maid,
Have you conspired, have you with these contrived,
To bait me with this foul derision?
Is all the counsel that we two have shared,
The sisters' vows, the hours that we have spent,
When we have chid the hasty-footed time   200
For parting us—O! is all forgot?
All school-days' friendship, childhood innocence?
We, Hermia, like two artificial gods,
Have with our needles created both one flower,
Both on one sampler, sitting on one cushion,
Both warbling of one song, both in one key;
As if our hands, our sides, voices, and minds,
Had been incorporate. So we grew together,
Like to a double cherry, seeming parted,
But yet an union in partition,   210
Two lovely berries moulded on one stem:
So, with two seeming bodies, but one heart,
Two of the first, like coats in heraldry,
Due but to one, and crownéd with one crest.
And will you rend our ancient love asunder,
To join with men in scorning your poor friend?
It is not friendly, 'tis not maidenly—
Our sex, as well as I, may chide you for it;
Though I alone do feel the injury.
  Hermia. Helen, I am amazéd at your words.   220
I scorn you not—it seems that you scorn me.
  Helena. Have you not set Lysander, as in scorn,

To follow me and praise my eyes and face?
And made your other love, Demetrius
(Who even but now did spurn me with his foot!)
To call me goddess, nymph, divine and rare,
Precious, celestial? Wherefore speaks he this
To her he hates? and wherefore doth Lysander
Deny your love (so rich within his soul)
230 And tender me (forsooth!) affection,
But by your setting on, by your consent?
What though I be not so in grace as you,
So hung upon with love, so fortunate,
But miserable most, to love unloved?
This you should pity rather than despise.

   Hermia. I understand not what you mean by this.
   Helena. Ay, do! perséver, counterfeit sad looks,
Make mouths upon me when I turn my back,
Wink at each other, hold the sweet jest up.
240 This sport, well carried, shall be chronicled.
If you have any pity, grace, or manners,
You would not make me such an argument.
But, fare ye well: 'tis partly my own fault:
Which death or absence soon shall remedy.

   Lysander. Stay, gentle Helena; hear my excuse,
My love, my life, my soul, fair Helena!
   Helena. O excellent!
   Hermia.   Sweet, do not scorn her so.
   Demetrius. If she cannot entreat, I can compel.
   Lysander. Thou canst compel no more than
        she entreat.
250 Thy threats have no more strength than her weak
        prayers.
Helen, I love thee—by my life I do;
I swear by that which I will lose for thee,
To prove him false that says I love thee not.

Demetrius. I say I love thee more than he can do.
Lysander. If thou say so, withdraw, and prove it too.
Demetrius. Quick, come,—
Hermia [staying him].   Lysander, whereto tends all this?
Lysander. Away, you Ethiop!
Hermia. No, no!
Demetrius [scoffs.] Ye'll
Seem to break loose! take on as you would follow!
But yet come not. You are a tame man, go!
Lysander. Hang off, thou cat, thou burr! vile thing,
    let loose;   260
Or I will shake thee from me like a serpent.
Hermia. Why are you grown so rude? what change.
    is this,
Sweet love?   *[she keeps her hold upon him*
Lysander.   Thy love! out, tawny Tartar, out!
Out, loathéd med'cine! O, hated potion, hence!
Hermia. Do you not jest?
Helena.   Yes, sooth: and so do you.
Lysander. Demetrius, I will keep my word with thee.
Demetrius. I would I had your bond, for I perceive
A weak bond holds you. I'll not trust you word.
Lysander. What? should I hurt her, strike her, kill
    her dead?
Although I hate her, I'll not harm her so.   270
Hermia. What? can you do me greater harm than hate?
Hate me! wherefore? O me, what news, my love!
Am not I Hermia? are not you Lysander?
I am as fair now as I was erewhile.
Since night you loved me; yet since night you left me.
Why then, you left me—O, the gods forbid!—
In earnest, shall I say?
Lysander.   Ay, by my life!

And never did desire to see thee more.
Therefore be out of hope, of question or doubt:
280 Be certain: nothing truer: 'tis no jest
That I do hate thee and love Helena.

Hermia [*to Helena*]. O me, you juggler, you canker-
blossom.
You thief of love! What! have you come by night
And stol'n my love's heart from him?

Helena.   Fine, i'faith!
Have you no modesty, no maiden shame,
No touch of bashfulness? What! will you tear
Impatient answers from my gentle tongue?
Fie, fie, you counterfeit, you puppet you!

Hermia. 'Puppet?' Why, so,—ay, that way goes
the game!
290 Now I perceive that she hath made compare
Between our statures; she hath urged her height;
And with her personage, her tall personage,
Her height, forsooth, she hath prevailed with him.
And are you grown so high in his esteem
Because I am so dwarfish and so low?
How low am I, thou painted maypole? speak;
How low am I? I am not yet so low,
But that my nails can reach unto thine eyes.

                      [*she makes towards her*

Helena. I pray you, though you mock me, gentlemen,
300 Let her not hurt me. I was never curst:
I have no gift at all in shrewishness:
I am a right maid for my cowardice:
Let her not strike me. You perhaps may think,
Because she is something lower than myself,
That I can match her.

Hermia.   Lower! hark, again.

Helena. Good Hermia, do not be so bitter with me.

I evermore did love you, Hermia,
Did ever keep your counsels, never wronged you;
Save that, in love unto Demetrius,
I told him of your stealth unto this wood.   310
He followed you; for love I followed him.
But he hath chid me hence, and threat'ned me
To strike me, spurn me; nay, to kill me too.
And now, so you will let me quiet go,
To Athens will I bear my folly back,
And follow you no further. Let me go.
You see how simple and how fond I am.
 Hermia. Why, get you gone. Who is't that
  hinders you?
 Helena. A foolish heart that I leave here behind.
 Hermia. What! with Lysander?
 Helena.   With Demetrius.   320
 Lysander. Be not afraid: she shall not harm thee,
  Helena.
 Demetrius. No, sir; she shall not, though you take
  her part.
 Helena. When she is angry, she is keen and shrewd.
She was a vixen when she went to school;
And though she be but little, she is fierce.
 Hermia. 'Little' again? nothing but 'low' and 'little'!
Why will you suffer her to flout me thus?
Let me come to her.
 Lysander.   Get you gone, you dwarf;
You minimus, of hind'ring knot-grass made;
You bead, you acorn.
 Demetrius.   You are too officious   330
In her behalf that scorns your services.
Let her alone; speak not of Helena;
Take not her part; [*he draws his sword*] for if thou
  dost intend

Never so little show of love to her,
Thou shalt aby it.
 Lysander [*also draws*].   Now she holds me not;
Now follow, if thou dar'st, to try whose right,
Of thine or mine, is most in Helena.
           [*he turns into the wood*
 Demetrius. Follow! nay, I'll go with thee, cheek by jowl.
            [*he hastens after*
 Hermia. You, mistress, all this coil is 'long of you:
Nay: go not back.
340 *Helena.*   I will not trust you, I,
Nor longer stay in your curst company.
Your hands than mine are quicker for a fray;
My legs are longer though to run away. [*she runs off*
 Hermia. I am amazed, and know not what to say.
           [*she follows slowly*
 Oberon [*to Puck*]. This is thy negligence. Still
  thou mistak'st,
Or else committ'st thy knaveries wilfully.
 Puck. Believe me, king of shadows, I mistook.
Did not you tell me I should know the man
By the Athenian garments he had on?
350 And so far blameless proves my enterprise
That I have 'nointed an Athenian's eyes:
And so far am I glad it so did sort,
As this their jangling I esteem a sport.
 Oberon. Thou see'st these lovers seek a place to fight:
Hie therefore, Robin, overcast the night,
The starry welkin cover thou anon
With drooping fog as black as Acheron,
And lead these testy rivals so astray,
As one come not within another's way.
360 Like to Lysander sometime frame thy tongue;
Then stir Demetrius up with bitter wrong;

And sometime rail thou like Demetrius:
And from each other look thou lead them thus;
Till o'er their brows death-counterfeiting sleep
With leaden legs and batty wings doth creep:
Then crush this herb into Lysander's eye;
Whose liquor hath this virtuous property,
To take from thence all error with his might,
And make his eyeballs roll with wonted sight.
When they next wake, all this derision   370
Shall seem a dream and fruitless vision,
And back to Athens shall the lovers wend
With league whose date till death shall never end.
Whiles I in this affair do thee employ,
I'll to my queen and beg her Indian boy;
And then I will her charméd eye release
From monster's view, and all things shall be peace.
    Puck. My fairy lord, this must be done with haste,
For night's swift dragons cut the clouds full fast;
And yonder shines Aurora's harbinger,   380
At whose approach ghosts wand'ring here and there,
Troop home to churchyards. Damnéd spirits all,
That in crossways and floods have burial,
Already to their wormy beds are gone;
For fear lest day should look their shames upon,
They wilfully themselves exile from light,
And must for aye consort with black-browed night.
    Oberon. But we are spirits of another sort.
I with the morning's love have oft made sport,
And like a forester the groves may tread,   390
Even till the eastern gate, all fiery-red,
Opening on Neptune with fair blesséd beams,
Turns into yellow gold his salt green streams.
But, notwithstanding, haste—make no delay:
We may effect this business yet ere day.   [*he goes*

A fog descends

Puck. Up and down, up and down,
I will lead them up and down.
I am feared in field and town.
Goblin, lead them up and down....

400 Here comes one.   [*he vanishes*

LYSANDER *returns, groping in the dark*

Lysander. Where art thou, proud Demetrius? speak
thou now.
Puck as Demetrius. Here, villain! drawn and ready.
Where art thou?
Lysander. I will be with thee straight.
The voice receding.   Follow me then
To plainer ground.   [*Lysander follows the voice*

DEMETRIUS *approaches, groping likewise*

Demetrius.   Lysander! speak again.
Thou runaway, thou coward, art thou fled?
Speak! In some bush? Where dost thou hide thy head?
Puck as Lysander. Thou coward, art thou bragging
to the stars,
Telling the bushes that thou look'st for wars,
And wilt not come? Come recreant, come thou child,
410 I'll whip thee with a rod. He is defiled
That draws a sword on thee.
Demetrius.   Yea, art thou there?
The voice receding. Follow my voice: we'll try no
manhood here.   [*Demetrius follows the voice*

LYSANDER *returns*

Lysander. He goes before me and still dares me on:
When I come where he calls, then he is gone.
The villain is much lighter-heeled than I:

I followed fast; but faster he did fly;
That fallen am I in dark uneven way,
And here will rest me....[*he lies down upon a bank*]
                              Come, thou gentle day,
For if but once thou show me thy grey light,
I'll find Demetrius and revenge this spite.   [*he sleeps* 420

DEMETRIUS *returns, running*

Puck as Lysander. Ho, ho, ho! Coward, why com'st
      thou not?
   Demetrius. Abide me if thou dar'st, for well
      I wot
Thou runn'st before me, shifting every place,
And dar'st not stand, nor look me in the face.
Where art thou now?
   The voice afar off.   Come hither; I am here.
   Demetrius. Nay, then thou mock'st me. Thou shalt
      buy this dear,
If ever I thy face by daylight see.
Now, go thy way. Faintness constraineth me
To measure out my length on this cold bed.
By day's approach look to be visited.   430
              [*he lies down upon another bank and sleeps*

HELENA *enters the clearing*

Helena. O weary night, O long and tedious night,
   Abate thy hours! Shine comforts from the east,
That I may back to Athens by daylight,
   From these that my poor company detest.
And sleep, that sometimes shuts up sorrow's eye,
Steal me awhile from mine own company.
                    [*she gropes her way to the bank where
                        Demetrius lies and falls asleep thereon*

PUCK reappears

Puck. Yet but three? Come one more.
Two of both kinds makes up four.
Here she comes, curst and sad.
440   Cupid is a knavish lad,
Thus to make poor females mad.

HERMIA returns, dejected

Hermia. Never so weary, never so in woe;
  Bedabbled with the dew and torn with briars;
I can no further crawl, no further go;
  My legs can keep no pace with my desires.
Here will I rest me till the break of day.
Heavens shield Lysander, if they mean a fray!
    [*she gropes her way to the bank on which Lysander
      lies and falls asleep*

    Puck. On the ground
      Sleep sound:
450   I'll apply
      To your eye,
    Gentle lover, remedy.
        [*he anoints Lysander's eyes with the*
      When thou wak'st,   *love-juice*
      Thou tak'st
      True delight
      In the sight
Of thy former lady's eye:
And the country proverb known,
That every man should take his own,
460 In your waking shall be shown.
      Jack shall have Jill;
      Nought shall go ill;
The man shall have his mare again, and all shall be well.
      [*he vanishes; the fog disperses*

[4.1.] *TITANIA approaches with* BOTTOM, *his ass's head garlanded with flowers; fairies follow in their train,* OBERON *behind all, unseen*

Titania. Come, sit thee down upon this flow'ry bed;
  While I thy amiable cheeks do coy,
And stick musk-roses in thy sleek smooth head,
  And kiss thy fair large ears, my gentle joy.

                             [*they sit; she embraces him*

Bottom. Where's Peaseblossom?

Peaseblossom. Ready.

Bottom. Scratch my head, Peaseblossom. Where's Monsieur Cobweb?

Cobweb. Ready.

Bottom. Monsieur Cobweb, good monsieur, get you 10 your weapons in your hand and kill me a red-hipped humble-bee on the top of a thistle; and, good monsieur, bring me the honey-bag. Do not fret yourself too much in the action, monsieur; and, good monsieur, have a care the honey-bag break not—I would be loath to have you overflown with a honey bag, signior. Where's Monsieur Mustardseed?

Mustardseed. Ready.

Bottom. Give me your neaf, Monsieur Mustardseed. Pray you, leave your curtsy, good monsieur. 20

Mustardseed. What's your will?

Bottom. Nothing, good monsieur, but to help Cavalery Cobweb to scratch. I must to the barber's, monsieur; for methinks I am marvellous hairy about the face—and I am such a tender ass, if my hair do but tickle me I must scratch.

Titania. What, wilt thou hear some music, my
    sweet love?

Bottom. I have a reasonable good ear in music. Let's have the tongs and the bones.

30   *Titania.* Or say, sweet love, what thou desir'st to eat.
   Bottom. Truly, a peck of provender. I could munch
your good dry oats. Methinks I have a great desire to
a bottle of hay. Good hay, sweet hay, hath no fellow.
   Titania. I have a venturous fairy, that shall seek
†The squirrel's hoard, and fetch thee thence new nuts.
   Bottom. I had rather have a handful or two of dried
peas. But, I pray you, let none of your people stir me;
I have an exposition of sleep come upon me.
   Titania. Sleep thou, and I will wind thee in
      my arms.
40 Fairies, be gone, and be all ways away.

                         [the fairies leave them
†So doth the woodbine the sweet honeysuckle
Gently entwist: the female ivy so
Enrings the barky fingers of the elm.
O, how I love thee! how I dote on thee!   *[they sleep*

      OBERON *draws nigh and looks upon them;*
             PUCK *appears*

   Oberon. Welcome, good Robin. See'st thou this
      sweet sight?
Her dotage now I do begin to pity.
For meeting her of late behind the wood,
Seeking sweet favours for this hateful fool,
I did upbraid her and fall out with her.
50 For she his hairy temples then had rounded
With coronet of fresh and fragrant flowers;
And that same dew which sometime on the buds
Was wont to swell like round and orient pearls
Stood now within the pretty flowerets' eyes
Like tears that did their own disgrace bewail.
When I had at my pleasure taunted her,
And she in mild terms begged my patience,

I then did ask of her her changeling child;
Which straight she gave me, and her fairy sent
To bear him to my bower in Fairyland.   60
And now I have the boy, I will undo
This hateful imperfection of her eyes.
And, gentle Puck, take this transforméd scalp
From off the head of this Athenian swain;
That he, awaking when the other do,
May all to Athens back again repair,
And think no more of this night's accidents
But as the fierce vexation of a dream.
But first I will release the Fairy Queen....
  Be as thou wast wont to be: [*he anoints her eyes* 70
  See, as thou wast wont to see.
  Dian's bud o'er Cupid's flower
  Hath such force and blesséd power.
Now, my Titania! wake you, my sweet queen.
 Titania. My Oberon! what visions have I seen!
Methought I was enamoured of an ass.
 Oberon. There lies your love.
 Titania.   How came these things to pass?
O, how mine eyes do loathe his visage now!
 Oberon. Silence, awhile. Robin, take off this head.
Titania, music call; and strike more dead   80
Than common sleep of all these five the sense.
 Titania. Music, ho! music! such as charmeth sleep.
               [*soft music*
 Puck. Now, when thou wak'st, with thine own fool's
  eyes peep. [*he plucks the ass's head from him*
 Oberon. Sound, music. [*the music waxes loud*] Come,
  my queen, take hands with me,
And rock the ground whereon these sleepers be.
               [*they dance*
Now thou and I are new in amity.

And will to-morrow midnight solemnly
Dance in Duke Theseus' house triumphantly,
And bless it to all fair prosperity.
90 There shall the pairs of faithful lovers be
Wedded, with Theseus, all in jollity.
  Puck. Fairy King, attend, and mark:
I do hear the morning lark.
  Oberon. Then, my queen, in silence sad,
Trip we after the night's shade:
We the globe can compass soon,
Swifter than the wand'ring moon.
  Titania. Come my lord, and in our flight,
Tell me how it came this night
100 That I sleeping here was found
With these mortals on the ground. [*they vanish*

*There is a sound of horns; THESEUS, HIPPOLYTA, EGEUS
and others are seen approaching, arrayed for the hunt*

 Theseus. Go, one of you, find out the forester;
For now our observation is performed,
And since we have the vaward of the day,
My love shall hear the music of my hounds.
Uncouple in the western valley, let them go:
Dispatch, I say, and find the forester.
        [*a servant bows and departs*
We will, fair queen, up to the mountain's top,
And mark the musical confusion
110 Of hounds and echo in conjunction.
 Hippolyta. I was with Hercules and Cadmus once,
When in a wood of Crete they bayed the bear
With hounds of Sparta: never did I hear
Such gallant chiding; for, besides the groves,
The skies, the fountains, every region near
Seemed all one mutual cry. I never heard

So musical a discord, such sweet thunder.

Theseus. My hounds are bred out of the Spartan kind:
So flewed, so sanded; and their heads are hung
With ears that sweep away the morning dew—   120
Crook-kneed, and dewlapped like Thessalian bulls;
Slow in pursuit; but matched in mouth like bells,
Each under each. A cry more tuneable
Was never hollaed to, nor cheered with horn,
In Crete, in Sparta, nor in Thessaly.
Judge when you hear. But, soft, what nymphs are these?

Egeus. My lord, this is my daughter here asleep—
And this Lysander—this Demetrius is—
This Helena, old Nedar's Helena.
I wonder of their being here together.   130

Theseus. No doubt they rose up early to observe
The rite of May; and, hearing our intent,
Came here in grace of our solemnity....
But, speak, Egeus; is not this the day
That Hermia should give answer of her choice?

Egeus. It is, my lord.

Theseus.   Go, bid the huntsmen wake them with
    their horns.

        [*horns, and a shout; the lovers awake and 'start up'*
Good morrow, friends. Saint Valentine is past;
Begin these wood-birds but to couple now?

Lysander. Pardon, my lord.   [*they kneel to Theseus*

Theseus.   I pray you all, stand up.   140
I know you two are rival enemies:
How comes this gentle concord in the world,
That hatred is so far from jealousy
To sleep by hate, and fear no enmity?

Lysander. My lord, I shall reply amazedly,
Half sleep, half waking....but as yet, I swear,
I cannot truly say how I came here....

But, as I think—for truly would I speak,
And now I do bethink me, so it is—
150 I came with Hermia hither. Our intent
Was to be gone from Athens...where we might,
Without the peril of the Athenian law—
    Egeus. Enough, enough, my lord; you have enough.
I beg the law, the law, upon his head.
They would have stol'n away, they would, Demetrius,
Thereby to have defeated you and me:
You of your wife, and me of my consent—
Of my consent that she should be your wife.
    Demetrius. My lord, fair Helen told me of their stealth
160 Of this their purpose hither to this wood,
And I in fury hither followed them;
Fair Helena in fancy following me.
But, my good lord, I wot not by what power—
But by some power it is—my love to Hermia,
Melted as melts the snow, seems to me now
As the remembrance of an idle gaud
Which in my childhood I did dote upon:
And all the faith, the virtue of my heart,
The object and the pleasure of mine eye,
170 Is only Helena. To her, my lord,
Was I betrothed ere I saw Hermia:
But, like in sickness, did I loathe this food,
So, as in health, come to my natural taste,
Now I do wish it, love it, long for it,
And will for evermore be true to it.
    Theseus. Fair lovers, you are fortunately met.
Of this discourse we more will hear anon.
Egeus, I will overbear your will;
For in the temple, by and by, with us,
180 These couples shall eternally be knit.
And, for the morning now is something worn,

Our purposed hunting shall be set aside.
Away with us, to Athens! Three and three,
We'll hold a feast in great solemnity.
Come, Hippolyta.

   [*Theseus, Hippolyta, Egeus and their train depart*
 Demetrius. These things seem small and undis-
   tinguishable,
Like far-off mountains turnéd into clouds.
 Hermia. Methinks I see these things with parted eye,
.When everything seems double.
 Helena.   So methinks:
And I have found Demetrius like a jewel,   190
Mine own, and not mine own.
 Demetrius.   Are you sure
That we are well awake? It seems to me,
That yet we sleep, we dream. Do not you think
The duke was here, and bid us follow him?
 Hermia. Yea, and my father.
 Helena.   And Hippolyta.
 Lysander. And he did bid us follow to the temple.
 Demetrius. Why then, we are awake; let's follow him;
And by the way let us recount our dreams.

        [*they follow Theseus*
 Bottom [*awaking*]. When my cue comes, call me, and
I will answer. My next is, 'Most fair Pyramus.' Heigh- 200
ho! [*he yawns, and looks about him*] Peter Quince! Flute,
the bellows-mender! Snout, the tinker! Starveling!
God's my life! stol'n hence, and left me asleep! I have
had a most rare vision. I have had a dream—past the
wit of man to say what dream it was. Man is but an
ass, if he go about to expound this dream. [*he rises*]
Methought I was—there is no man can tell what....[*he
passes his hand across his head, touching his ears*] Methought I was, and methought I had....but man is but a

210 patched fool, if he will offer to say what methought I
had. The eye of man hath not heard, the ear of man
hath not seen, man's hand is not able to taste, his tongue
to conceive, nor his heart to report, what my dream was.
I will get Peter Quince to write a ballad of this dream:
it shall be called Bottom's Dream; because it hath no
bottom: and I will sing it in the latter end of our play,
before the duke. Peradventure, to make it the more
gracious, I shall sing it at her death.   [*he goes*

[4.2.]   *The room in Peter Quince's cottage*

QUINCE, FLUTE, SNOUT *and* STRAVELING

Quince. Have you sent to Bottom's house? is he come
home yet?

Starveling. He cannot be heard of. Out of doubt he
is transported.

Flute. If he come not, then the play is marred. It goes
not forward, doth it?

Quince. It is not possible. You have not a man in all
Athens able to discharge Pyramus but he.

Flute. No, he hath simply the best wit of any handicraft
10 man in Athens.

Quince. Yea, and the best person too—and he is a very
paramour for a sweet voice.

Flute. You must say 'paragon'. A paramour is, God
bless us! a thing of naught.

SNUG *enters*

Snug. Masters, the duke is coming from the temple, and
there is two or three lords and ladies more married—if
our sport had gone forward, we had all been made men.

Flute. O sweet bully Bottom! Thus hath he lost sixpence
a day during his life: he could not have 'scaped sixpence

a day. An the duke had not given him sixpence a day
for playing Pyramus, I'll be hanged. He would have
deserved it: sixpence a day in Pyramus, or nothing.

BOTTOM enters   20

Bottom. Where are these lads? where are these hearts?
Quince. Bottom! O most courageous day! O most
happy hour!   [*they all crowd about him*
Bottom. Masters, I am to discourse wonders: but ask
me not what; for if I tell you, I am not true Athenian.
I will tell you every thing, right as it fell out.
Quince. Let us hear, sweet Bottom.
Bottom. Not a word of me. All that I will tell you is,   30
that the duke hath dined. Get your apparel together—
good strings to your beards, new ribbons to your pumps—
meet presently at the palace, every man look o'er his
part; for the short and the long is, our play is preferred.
In any case, let Thisby have clean linen; and let not
him that plays the lion pare his nails; for they shall hang
out for the lion's claws....And, most dear actors, eat no
onions nor garlic; for we are to utter sweet breath; and
I do not doubt but to hear them say, it is a sweet comedy.
No more words....away, go away!   [*they hurry forth*   40

[5.1.] *The hall in the palace of Duke Theseus. A
curtain conceals the entrance to the lobby at the back.
A fire burns upon the hearth. Lights and torches*

*THESEUS and HIPPOLYTA enter, followed
by PHILOSTRATE, lords and attendants.
The Duke and Duchess take their seats*

Hippolyta. 'Tis strange, my Theseus, that these lovers
    speak of.
Theseus. More strange than true. I never may believe

These antic fables, nor these fairy toys.
Lovers and madmen have such seething brains,
Such shaping fantasies, that apprehend
More than cool reason ever comprehends.
The lunatic, the lover, and the poet,
Are of imagination all compact.
One sees more devils than vast hell can hold;
10 That is, the madman. The lover, all as frantic,
Sees Helen's beauty in a brow of Egypt.
The poet's eye, in a fine frenzy rolling,
Doth glance from heaven to earth, from earth to heaven;
And as imagination bodies forth
The forms of things unknown, the poet's pen
Turns them to shapes, and gives to airy nothing
A local habitation and a name.
Such tricks hath strong imagination
That, if it would but apprehend some joy,
20 It comprehends some bringer of that joy;
Or in the night, imagining some fear,
How easy is a bush supposed a bear!
   Hippolyta. But all the story of the night told over,
And all their minds transfigured so together,
More witnesseth than fancy's images,
And grows to something of great constancy—
But howsoever strange and admirable.
   Theseus. Here come the lovers, full of joy
       and mirth.

LYSANDER *and* **HERMIA,** **DEMETRIUS** *and* **HELENA**
    enter, laughing and talking together

Joy, gentle friends! joy and fresh days of love
30 Accompany your hearts!
   Lysander.   More than to us
Wait in your royal walks, your board, your bed!

Theseus. Come now; what masques, what dances shall
we have,
To wear away this long age of three hours
Between our after-supper and bed-time?
Where is our usual manager of mirth?
What revels are in hand? Is there no play
To ease the anguish of a torturing hour?
Call Philostrate.
Philostrate. Here, mighty Theseus.
Theseus. Say, what abridgment have you for this
evening?
What masque? what music? How shall we beguile   40
The lazy time, if not with some delight?
Philostrate. There is a brief how many sports
are ripe;
Make choice of which your highness will see first.
                           [he presents a paper
Theseus. 'The battle with the Centaurs, to be sung,
By an Athenian eunuch to the harp.'
We'll none of that: that have I told my love,
In glory of my kinsman Hercules.
'The riot of the tipsy Bacchanals,
Tearing the Thracian singer in their rage'
That is an old device; and it was played   50
When I from Thebes came last a conqueror.
'The thrice three Muses mourning for the death
Of Learning, late deceased in beggary.'
That is some satire, keen and critical,
Not sorting with a nuptial ceremony.
'A tedious brief scene of young Pyramus
And his love Thisby; very tragical mirth.'
Merry and tragical! tedious and brief!
†That is hot ice and wondrous strange snow.
How shall we find the concord of this discord?   60

Philostrate. A play there is, my lord, some ten
    words long;
Which is as brief as I have known a play;
But by ten words, my lord, it is too long;
Which makes it tedious: for in all the play
There is not one word apt, one player fitted.
And tragical, my noble lord, it is;
For Pyramus therein doth kill himself.
Which when I saw rehearsed, I must confess,
Made mine eyes water; but more merry tears
70 The passion of loud laughter never shed.
    Theseus. What are they that do play it?
    Philostrate. Hard-handed men that work in
    Athens here,
Which never laboured in their minds till now;
And now have toiled their unbreathed memories
With this same play against your nuptial.
    Theseus. And we will hear it.
    Philostrate.   No, my noble lord,
It is not for you: I have heard it over,
And it is nothing, nothing in the world;
Unless you can find sport in their intents,
80 Extremely stretched and conned with cruel pain,
To do you service.
    Theseus.   I will hear that play:
For never anything can be amiss,
When simpleness and duty tender it.
Go bring them in; and take your places, ladies.

          [Philostrate departs; the rest of the court
               make ready to hear the play

    Hippolyta. I love not to see wretchedness o'ercharged,
And duty in his service perishing.
    Theseus. Why, gentle sweet, you shall see no
    such thing.

Hippolyta. He says they can do nothing in this kind.
Theseus. The kinder we, to give them thanks
  for nothing.
Our sport shall be to take what they mistake: 90
And what poor duty cannot do, noble respect
Takes it in might not merit.
Where I have come, great clerks have puposéd
To greet me with premeditated welcomes;
Where I have seen them shiver and look pale,
Make periods in the midst of sentences,
Throttle their practised accent in their fears,
And in conclusion dumbly have broke off,
Not paying me a welcome. Trust me, sweet,
Out of this silence yet I picked a welcome;   100
And in the modesty of fearful duty
I read as much as from the rattling tongue
Of saucy and audacious eloquence.
Love, therefore, and tongue-tied simplicity
In least speak most, to my capacity.

Philostrate returns

Philostrate. So please your grace, the Prologue is
  addressed.
Theseus. Let him approach.

Enter before the curtain QUINCE for the Prologue

Quince. 'If we offend, it is with our good will.
 That you should think, we come not to offend,
But with good will. To show our simple skill,   110
 That is the true beginning of our end.
Consider then, we come but in despite.
 We do not come, as minding to content you,
Our true intent is. All for your delight
 We are not here. That you should here repent you,

The actors are at hand: and, by their show,
You shall know all, that you are like to know,'

        [he whips behind the curtain

Theseus. This fellow doth not stand upon points.

Lysander. He hath rid his prologue like a rough colt:
120 he knows not the stop. A good moral, my lord—it is not
enough to speak; but to speak true.

Hippolyta. Indeed he hath played on his prologue like
a child on a recorder—a sound, but not in government.

Theseus. His speech was like a tangled chain; nothing
impaired, but all disordered. Who is next?

Enter before the curtain PYRAMUS *and* THISBY, WALL,
MOONSHINE, *and* LION, *as in dumb-show, with* QUINCE
for the Presenter

  Quince. 'Gentles, perchance you wonder at this show,
    But wonder on, till truth make all things plain.
This man is Pyramus, if you would know:
    This beauteous lady Thisby is certain.
130 This man, with lime and rough-cast, doth present
    Wall, that vile Wall which did these lovers sunder:
And through Wall's chink, poor souls, they are content
    To whisper. At the which let no man wonder.
This man, with lantern, dog, and bush of thorn,
    Presenteth Moonshine. For, if you will know,
By moonshine did these lovers think no scorn
    To meet at Ninus' tomb, there, there to woo:
This grisly beast (which Lion hight by name)
    The trusty Thisby, coming first by night,
140 Did scare away, or rather did affright:
    And, as she fled, her mantle she did fall:
Which Lion vile with bloody mouth did stain.
Anon comes Pyramus, sweet youth, and tall,
    And finds his trusty Thisby's mantle slain:

Whereat, with blade, with bloody blameful blade,
  He bravely broached his boiling bloody breast.
And Thisby, tarrying in mulberry shade,
  His dagger drew, and died. For all the rest,
Let Lion, Moonshine, Wall, and lovers twain,
At large discourse, while here they do remain.'   150

Theseus. I wonder if the lion be to speak.

Demetrius. No wonder, my lord: one lion may, when many asses do.   [*exeunt all save Wall and Pyramus*

WALL *steps forward*

Wall. 'In this same interlude it doth befall
That I, one Snout by name, present a wall:
And such a wall, as I would have you think,
That had in it a crannied hole or chink:
Through which the lovers, Pyramus and Thisby,
Did whisper often very secretly....
This loam, this rough-cast, and this stone, doth show   160
That I am that same wall; the truth is so.
And this the cranny is, right and sinister,
                              [*he stretches forth his fingers*
Through which the fearful lovers are to whisper.'

Theseus. Would you desire lime and hair to speak better?

Demetrius. It is the wittiest partition that ever I heard discourse, my lord.

PYRAMUS *steps forward*

Theseus. Pyramus draws near the wall: silence!

Pyramus. 'O grim-looked night! O night with hue
    so black!
  O night, which ever art when day is not: 170
O night, O night, alack, alack, alack,
  I fear my Thisby's promise is forgot!

And thou, O wall! O sweet, O lovely wall!
 That stand'st between her father's ground and mine,
Thou wall, O wall! O sweet and lovely wall!
 Show me thy chink to blink through with mine eyne.

                                                    [*Wall obeys*

Thanks, courteous wall. Jove shield thee well for this!
 But what see I? No Thisby do I see.
O wicked wall, through whom I see no bliss,
180   Cursed be thy stones for thus deceiving me!'
  Theseus. The wall, methinks, being sensible, should
curse again.
  Pyramus. No, in truth, sir, he should not. 'Deceiving
me' is Thisby's cue: she is to enter now, and I am to spy
her through the wall. You shall see, it will fall pat as
I told you. Yonder she comes.

Enter THISBY

  Thisby. 'O wall! full often hast thou heard my moans,
 For parting my fair Pyramus and me.
My cherry lips have often kissed thy stones;
190   Thy stones with lime and hair knit up in thee.'
  Pyramus. 'I see a voice: now will I to the chink,
 To spy an I can hear my Thisby's face.
Thisby!'
  Thisby.   'My love! thou art my love, I think.'
  Pyramus. 'Think what thou wilt, I am thy
            lover's grace;
And, like Limander, am I trusty still.'
  Thisby. 'And I like Helen, till the Fates me kill.'
  Pyramus. 'Not Shafalus to Procrus was so true.'
  Thisby. 'As Shafalus to Procrus, I to you.'
  Pyramus. 'O! kiss me through the hole of this
            vile wall.'
200 *Thisby.* 'I kiss the wall's hole, not your lips at all.'

Pyramus. 'Wilt thou at Ninny's tomb meet me
    straightway?'

Thisby. ''Tide life, 'tide death, I come without delay.'
                      [exeunt Pyramus and Thisby

Wall. 'Thus have I, Wall, my part dischargéd so;
And being done, thus Wall away doth go.'   *[exit Wall*

Theseus. Now is the mural down between the two
neighbours.

Demetrius. No remedy, my lord, when walls are so
wilful to hear without warning.

Hippolyta. This is the silliest stuff that ever I heard.

Theseus. The best in this kind are but shadows: and   210
the worst are no worse, if imagination amend them.

Hippolyta. It must be your imagination then; and
not theirs.

Theseus. If we imagine no worse of them than they of
themselves, they may pass for excellent men. Here
come two noble beasts, in a moon and a lion.

Enter Lion and Moonshine

Lion. 'You ladies, you, whose gentle hearts do fear
  The smallest monstrous mouse that creeps on floor,
May now perchance both quake and tremble here,
  When lion rough in wildest rage doth roar.   220
Then know that I, as Snug the joiner am
A lion fell, nor else no lion's dam.
For if I should as lion come in strife
Into this place, 'twere pity on my life.'

Theseus. A very gentle beast, and of a good con-
science.

Demetrius. The very best at a beast, my lord, that e'er
I saw.

Lysander. This lion is a very fox for his valour.

Theseus. True: and a goose for his discretion.   230

Demetrius. Not so, my lord, for his valour cannot carry his discretion; and the fox carries the goose.

Theseus. His discretion, I am sure, cannot carry his valour, for the goose carries not the fox. It is well: leave it to his discretion, and let us listen to the moon.

Moonshine. 'This lanthorn doth the hornéd moon
    present'—

Demetrius. He should have worn the horns on his head.

240 *Theseus.* He is no crescent, and his horns are invisible within the circumference.

Moonshine. 'This lanthorn doth the hornéd moon
    present,
Myself the man i'th' moon do seem to be.'

Theseus. This is the greatest error of all the rest: the man should be put into the lantern. How is it else the man i'th' moon?

Demetrius. He dares not come there for the candle—for, you see, it is already in snuff.

Hippolyta. I am aweary of this moon. Would he
250 would change!

Theseus. It appears, by his small light of discretion, that he is in the wane: but yet, in courtesy, in all reason, we must stay the time.

Lysander. Proceed, Moon.

Moonshine. All that I have to say, is to tell you that the lanthorn is the moon, I the man i'th' moon, this thorn-bush my thorn-bush, and this dog my dog.

Demetrius. Why, all these should be in the lantern; for all these are in the moon. But, silence; here
260 comes Thisby.

*Enter THISBY; LION and MOONSHINE draw
back the curtain before the lobby, discovering
a placard within inscribed NINUS' TOMB*

Thisby. 'This is old Ninny's tomb. Where is my love?'
Lion [*roars*]. 'Oh'—

     [*Thisby casts her mantle from her and runs away*
Demetrius. Well roared, Lion.
Theseus. Well run, Thisby.
Hippolyta. Well shone, Moon. Truly, the moon shines
with a good grace.   [*Lion paws Thisby's mantle*
Theseus. Well moused, Lion.
Demetrius. And then came Pyramus.

Enter PYRAMUS; exit LION

Lysander. And so the lion vanished.
Pyramus. 'Sweet moon, I thank thee for thy
    sunny beams.   **270**
 I thank thee, moon, for shining now so bright.
For, by thy gracious, golden, glittering gleams,
    I trust to take of truest Thisby sight.
        But stay...O spite!
        But mark, poor knight,
    What dreadful dole is here!
        Eyes, do you see?
        How can it be?
    O dainty duck, O dear!
        Thy mantle good,   **280**
        What, stained with blood?
    Approach, ye Furies fell!
        O Fates, come, come,
        Cut thread and thrum,
    Quail, crush, conclude, and quell!'
Theseus. This passion—and the death of a dear friend—
would go near to make a man look sad.

Hippolyta. Beshrew my heart, but I pity the man.

Pyramus. 'O wherefore, Nature, didst thou
    lions frame?

290   Since lion vile hath here deflowered my dear.
Which is—no, no—which was the fairest dame
    That lived, that loved, that liked, that looked
        with cheer.
            Come, tears, confound;
            Out, sword, and wound
        The pap of Pyramus:
            Ay, that left pap,
            Where heart doth hop.... *[he stabs himself*
    Thus die I, thus, thus, thus....
           *[he drops the sword and staggers across the
              floor to fall within the tomb*
            Now am I dead,
300   Now am I fled,
My soul is in the sky.
            Tongue, lose thy light!
            Moon, take thy flight!   *[exit Moonshine*
Now die, die, die, die, die.' *[he muffles his face*

Demetrius. No die, but an ace, for him—for he is but
one.

Lysander. Less than an ace, man—for he is dead,
he is nothing.

Theseus. With the help of a surgeon, he might yet
310 recover, and prove an ass.

Hippolyta. How chance Moonshine is gone before
Thisby comes back and finds her lover?

Theseus. She will find him by starlight. Here she
comes, and her passion ends the play.

Enter THISBY

Hippolyta. Methinks she should not use a long one
for such a Pyramus: I hope she will be brief.

Demetrius. A mote will turn the balance, which
Pyramus, which Thisby, is the better: he for a man,
God warr'nt us; she for a woman, God bless us.

Lysander. She hath spied him already with those sweet 320
eyes.   [*Thisby discovers Pyramus in the tomb*

Demetrius. And thus she means, videlicet:—

   Thisby. 'Asleep, my love?

       What, dead, my dove?

  O Pyramus, arise,

       Speak, speak. Quite dumb?

                     [*she uncovers his face*

       Dead, dead? A tomb

  Must cover thy sweet eyes.

       These lily lips,

       This cherry nose,   330

  These yellow cowslip cheeks,

       Are gone, are gone:

       Lovers, make moan:

  His eyes were green as leeks.

       O Sisters Three,

       Come, come, to me,

  With hands as pale as milk;

       Lay them in gore,

       Since you have shore

  With shears his thread of silk.   340

       Tongue, not a word:

       Come, trusty sword,

  Come, blade, my breast imbrue...

      [*she searches Pyramus for the sword and not
         finding it stabs herself perforce with the
         scabbard*

  And farewell, friends:

       Thus Thisby ends:

  Adieu, adieu, adieu.'

              [*she falls heavily across the body*

Enter LION, MOONSHINE *and* WALL; *they close
the curtain before "Ninny's tomb"*

Theseus. Moonshine and Lion are left to bury the
dead.

Demetrius. Ay, and Wall too.

350 *Lion.* No, I assure you, the wall is down that parted
their fathers. [*he plucks a paper from his bosom*] Will it
please you to see the Epilogue, or to hear a Bergomask
dance between two of our company?

Theseus. No Epilogue, I pray you—for your play needs
no excuse. Never excuse; for when the players are all
dead, there need none to be blamed. Marry, if he that
writ it had played Pyramus and hanged himself in
Thisby's garter, it would have been a fine tragedy: and
so it is truly, and very notably discharged....But come,
360 your Bergomask: let your Epilogue alone.

MOONSHINE *and* WALL *dance the Bergomask and go out;*
THESEUS *rises*

The iron tongue of midnight hath told twelve!
Lovers, to bed—'tis almost fairy time.
I fear we shall out-sleep the coming morn,
As much as we this night have overwatched.
This palpable-gross play hath well beguiled
The heavy gait of night. Sweet friends, to bed.
A fortnight hold we this solemnity,
In nightly revels, and new jollity.

*The Duke leads Hippolyta forth, followed by the lovers,
hand in hand, and the rest of the court; the lights are
extinguished and all is dark, save for the dying embers
on the hearth*

Puck appears, broom in hand

Puck. Now the hungry lion roars,
   And the wolf behowls the moon;   370
Whilst the heavy ploughman snores,
   All with weary task fordone.
Now the wasted brands do glow,
   Whilst the screech-owl, screeching loud,
Puts the wretch that lies in woe
   In remembrance of a shroud.
Now it is the time of night,
   That the graves, all gaping wide,
Every one lets forth his sprite,
   In the church-way paths to glide.   380
And we fairies, that do run
   By the triple Hecate's team
From the presence of the sun,
   Following darkness like a dream,
Now are frolic. Not a mouse
Shall disturb this hallowed house....
I am sent with broom before,
To sweep the dust behind the door.

Of a sudden OBERON, TITANIA *and the fairy-host
stream into the hall, with rounds of waxen tapers
on their heads, which they swiftly kindle at the
hearth as they pass it by, until the great chamber
is full of light*

Oberon. Through the house give glimmer-
      ing light,
   By the dead and drowsy fire;   390
Every elf and fairy sprite
   Hop as light as bird from briar;
And this ditty after me
Sing, and dance it trippingly.

Titania [to Oberon]. First rehearse your
  song by rote,
To each word a warbling note;
Hand in hand, with fairy grace,
Will we sing and bless this place.

OBERON *leads and all the Fairies sing in chorus; as
they sing, they take hands and dance about the hall*

The Song

  Now, until the break of day,
400 Through this house each fairy stray.
  To the best bride-bed will we:
  Which by us shall blesséd be:
  And the issue, there create
  Ever shall be fortunate:
  So shall all the couples three
  Ever true in loving be:
  And the blots of Nature's hand
  Shall not in their issue stand.
  Never mole, hare-lip, nor scar,
410 Nor mark prodigious, such as are
  Despiséd in nativity,
  Shall upon their children be.
  With this field-dew consecrate,
  Every fairy take his gait,
  And each several chamber bless,
  Through this palace, with sweet peace;
  And the owner of it blest
  Ever shall in safety rest.
    Trip away:
420   Make no stay:
  Meet me all by break of day.

They pass out: the hall is dark and silent once again

Epilogue

spoken by Puck

If we shadows have offended,
Think but this, and all is mended,
That you have but slumb'red here
While these visions did appear.
And this weak and idle theme,
No more yielding but a dream,
Gentles, do not reprehend.
If you pardon, we will mend.
And, as I am an honest Puck,   430
If we have unearnéd luck
Now to 'scape the serpent's tongue,
We will make amends, ere long:
Else the Puck a liar call.
So, good night unto you all.
Give me your hands, if we be friends:
And Robin shall restore amends.

                              [*he vanishes*

THE COPY FOR
A MIDSUMMER-NIGHT'S DREAM, 1600

A. *The Fisher Quarto* (1600), *the Jaggard Quarto* (1619), *and the Folio text*

All scholars are now agreed that the *editio princeps* of the play in this volume is the quarto published in 1600 by Thomas Fisher. A moment's attention, however, is due to another quarto, printed according to its title-page 'by Iames Roberts, 1600,' and obviously set up from a copy of Fisher's edition, which indeed it imitates typographically with striking, not to say suspicious, fidelity. The existence of this remarkable reprint, belonging on the face of it to the same year as its predecessor, though evidently from a different printing-house, had long been one of the standing puzzles of Shakespearian textual criticism, when in 1906–9, by what ranks as the most brilliant and convincing feat of modern bibliography, Professor A. W. Pollard and Dr W. W. Greg were able to prove that the book, so far from being 'printed by Iames Roberts, 1600,' was actually printed, together with eight other Shakespearian or pseudo-Shakespearian texts, by William Jaggard in 1619[1]. It was in fact a fake, and editors might altogether disregard it from henceforth, did it not claim a small niche in the temple of fame as the link between the Fisher Quarto and the Folio version. In other words, Jaggard's compositors in 1623 used one of Jaggard's 1619 books as 'copy,' and it follows that the Folio version of this play is in substance only the reprint of a reprint, which not merely

---

[1] v. *Shakespeare Folios and Quartos*, 1909, ch. iv. We shall have more to say upon this matter in the next volume of the edition.

transmits most of the printer's errors of 1619 but also adds on its own account the usual crop of fresh errors that we expect in a Folio text taken from a quarto. Nevertheless, the 1623 edition possesses a considerable interest of its own, since it contains alterations which prove that the copy of the Jaggard Quarto from which it was set up had either itself served as a playhouse prompt-book or had been 'corrected,' for the purpose of publication, by some scribe working with the prompt-book before him. Most of the alterations, derived in this way from the prompter, affect the stage-directions. A few, however, concern the dialogue, though none, as we hope to show, can claim direct Shakespearian authority, which belongs to the Fisher Quarto alone. But for these matters the reader is referred to pp. 154–59, where the problems of the Folio text are considered in detail.

B. *The publication and printing of the Fisher Quarto*

Shakespeare's *Midsummer-Night's Dream* was first published late in 1600, presumably shortly after the following entry was made in the Stationers' Register:

1600] 8 octobris. Thomas ffyssher. Entred for his copie vnder the handes of master Rodes and the Wardens A booke called A mydsommer nightes Dreame. vj^d.

Practically nothing is known about those responsible for the production of the book. Thomas Fisher, originally a draper, was first admitted freeman of the Stationers' Company in June, 1600, and the only two books entered to him in the Register are *A Midsummer-Night's Dream* and, a year later, Marston's *Antonio and Mellida*, which he shared with another publisher[1]. Of the printer we know still less, seeing that his name has never even been identified. But though much is unknown, nothing is

---

[1] McKerrow, *Dict. of Printers*, Bib. Soc. Pub. 1910.

suspicious; the title-page looks honest enough, and the entry in the Stationers' Register is entirely and re-assuringly regular. Everything indicates that the pub-lisher procured his 'copy' from the Globe theatre in the ordinary way of business.

Of the Quarto as a piece of printer's craftsmanship there is fortunately little to record. Clark and Wright describe it as 'carelessly printed' in their *Cambridge Shakespeare* of 1863, but though it is superficially less accomplished than the 1619 reprint, it is superior to many of the other quartos, and decidedly better than *Love's Labour's Lost,* 1598, which was last con-sidered in this edition. The misprints are few, and the 'literals' fewer. The compositors seem to have worked slowly, whether through inexperience or because they found the manuscript difficult to read; for the text con-tains a number of interesting archaic spellings which almost certainly derive from the 'copy,' though they are nothing like so numerous as those supplied us by the prentice-compositor of *Love's Labour's Lost.* On the whole the work must be pronounced as moderately com-petent. Its chief weaknesses are two. First it is evident that the compositors conceived it their duty to expand most of the contractions they found in the original. Par-ticularly instructive in this connexion is the misprint 'Bet it' (2. 2. 47) in which we catch the compositor red-handed so to speak (cf. also notes 1. 1. 27, 69; 3. 1. 77; 3. 2. 204). And secondly it is clear that the compositors have introduced a large number of full stops into a text which originally contained very few, and that they have also peppered the dialogue with superfluous commas. Furthermore their pointing is care-less, as is shown by the numerous instances of trans-position in terminal stops. Nevertheless, apart from commas and periods the punctuation of the Quarto is comparatively good on the whole, at times even beautiful, and we have been able to follow it pretty closely.

C. *The manuscript*

The Fisher Quarto was beyond doubt printed from a theatrical prompt-book. Stage-directions, for example, such as 'Enter the King of Fairies, at one doore, with his traine; and the Queene, at another, with hers,' transport us at once from the forest of Shakespeare's Attica to the boards of his playhouse; while in others like 'Ly doune,' 'Sleepe' and 'Winde horne,' we hear the managerial voice giving real 'directions' to the players. Further, seeing that the Quarto contains a number of irregularities strongly suggestive of an author's manuscript, it seems not unnatural to suppose that here, as with *Much Ado*, 1600, and *Love's Labour's Lost*, 1598, we are once again confronted with a text printed directly from the prompt-book just as Shakespeare left it. We shall, at any rate, not hesitate to assume in what follows that the 'copy' for *A Midsummer-Night's Dream*, 1600, was actually Shakespeare's autograph manuscript, and we are in hopes that, when we have said our say, the reader will think the assumption a justifiable one.

(i) *A page of Shakespearian copy.*

In earlier volumes of this edition we have frequently drawn attention to the value of irregular verse-lining as a clue to the history of dramatic texts. A very beautiful illustration of the kind occurs at the beginning of Act 5 of the present play. The passage is here printed just as it appears in the Quarto, except that the disarranged verse has been italicised and slanting strokes inserted to show where the lines should rightly end.

5. 1. 1-84.

Enter Thefeus, Hyppolita, and Philoftrate.

Hip. Tis ftrange, my Thefeus, that thefe louers fpeake of.
The. More ftraunge then true. I neuer may beleeue
Thefe antique fables, nor thefe Fairy toyes.
Louers, and mad men haue fuch feething braines,

Such shaping phantasies, that apprehend/more,   5
Then coole reason euer comprehends./The lunatick,
The louer, and the Poet/are of imagination all compact./
One sees more diuels, then vast hell can holde:
That is the mad man. The louer, all as frantick,   10
Sees Helens beauty in a brow of Ægypt.
The Poets eye, in a fine frenzy, rolling,/doth glance
From heauen to earth, from earth to heauen./And as
Imagination bodies forth/the formes of things
Vnknowne: the Poets penne/turnes them to shapes,   15
And giues to ayery nothing,/a locall habitation,
*And a name./*Such trickes hath strong imagination,
That if it would but apprehend some ioy,
It comprehends some bringer of that ioy.   20
Or in the night, imagining some feare,
How easie is a bush suppos'd a Beare?
   Hyp. But, all the story of the night told ouer,
And all their minds transfigur'd so together,
More witnesseth than fancies images,   25
And growes to something of great constancy:
But howsoeuer, strange and admirable.

      Enter Louers; Lysander, Demetrius, Hermia and
                        Helena.

   The. Here come the louers, full of ioy and mirth.
Ioy, gentle friends, ioy and fresh daies
Of loue/accompany your hearts.
   Lys. More then to vs,/waite in your royall walkes, your 30
boorde, your bedde.   (haue,
   The. Come now: what maskes, what daunces shall wee
To weare away this long age of three hours,/betweene
Or¹ after supper, & bed-time?/Where is our vsuall manager
Of mirth?/What Reuels are in hand? Is there no play,/   35
To ease the anguish of a torturing hower?/Call Philostrate.
   Philostrate. Here mighty Theseus.
   The. Say, what abridgement haue you for this euening?
What maske, what musicke? How shall we beguile   40
The lazy tyme, if not with some delight?
   Philost. There is a briefe, how many sports are ripe.
Make choyce, of which your Highnesse will see first.
   The. The battell with the Centaures to be sung,

                    ¹ i.e. 'Our'

By an Athenian Eunuche, to the Harpe?   45
Weele none of that. That haue I tolde my loue,
In glory of my kinſman Hercules.
The ryot of the tipſie Bachanals,
Tearing the Thracian ſinger, in their rage?
That is an olde deuiſe: and it was plaid,   50
When I from Thebes came laſt a conqueror.
The thriſe three Muſes, mourning for the death
Of learning, late deceaſt, in beggery?
That is ſome Satire keene and criticall,
Not ſorting with a nuptiall ceremony.   55
A tedious briefe Scene of young Pyramus
And his loue Thiſby; very tragicall mirth?
Merry, and tragicall? Tedious, and briefe?/That is hot Iſe,
And wodrous[1] *ſtrange ſnow./How ſhall we find the cōcord*
Of this diſcord?   60
   Philoſt. A play there is, my Lord, ſome ten words long;
Which is as briefe, as I haue knowne a play:
But, by ten words, my Lord it is too long:
Which makes it tedious. For in all the Play,
There is not one word apt, one player fitted.   65
And tragicall, my noble Lord, it is./For Pyramus,
Therein, doth kill himſelfe./Which when I ſaw
Rehearſt, I muſt confeſſe,/made mine eyes water:
But more merry teares/the paſſion of loud laughter
Neuer ſhed./   70
   Theſe. What are they, that doe play it?
   Phil. Hard handed men, that worke in Athens here,
Which neuer labour'd in their minds till now:
And now haue toyled their vnbreathed memories,
With this ſame Play, againſt your nuptiall.   75
   The. And wee will heare it.
   Phil. No, my noble Lord,/*it is not for you. I haue heard*
It ouer,/and it is nothing, nothing in the world;/
Vnleſſe you can find ſport in their entents,
Extreamely ſtretcht, and cond with cruell paine,   80
To do you ſeruice.
   The. I will heare that play./*For neuer any thing*
Can be amiſſe,/when ſimpleneſſe and duety tender it./
Goe bring them in, and take your places, Ladies.

[1] i.e. 'wōdrous'

How came the compositor to divide the verse incorrectly in these eighty-four lines? And why should he go wrong in fits, so to speak; running smoothly enough 'in the even road of blank verse' for parts of the way, but on eight separate occasions suddenly swerving aside for a line or two? Submit the passage to a very simple operation; read it through, omitting the lines italicised in our transcript; and the responsibility for the eccentric verse-lining is seen to belong not to the compositor but in some way or other to Shakespeare himself. For what is left after the twenty-nine lines in italics have been dissected out are fifty-five lines of regularly divided verse, which are complete in themselves both in sense and metre, and must clearly, at some stage in the history of the text, have stood by themselves and run continuously[1]. Nevertheless, though the eight patches of disarranged verse are unnecessary to the bare sense, they contain all the beauty, all the life, all the memorable things of the passage. They are in our view mature Shakespearian verse, and their masterly diction and vigorous sweep, which pays no attention to line-termination but runs on 'until the idea which impels it is exhausted, introduce a note of intellectual energy that makes the whole glow with poetic genius. The remaining fifty-five lines, on the other hand, are simple, metrically regular, antithetical, end-stopped and just a little monotonous—in a word early Shakespearian verse. Indeed, the last two lines of Theseus' first speech are so poor that they have even been regarded as an interpolation by some critics[2].

And the dramatic contrast between the roman and the

---

[1] It is of course possible that some of the original draft was deleted when the additions were made; e.g. the fact that ll. 19–20 seem to echo ll. 5–6 (note 'apprehend... comprehend') has suggested to Dr W. W. Greg that the latter took the place of cancelled matter containing the same idea less admirably expressed.

[2] v. note 5. 1. 21–2.

italic lines is quite as remarkable as the poetic. The
lovers enter, and Theseus announces them (to the
audience) in a single line—and there an end, as far as
the version in roman print goes. It is the three lines
following in italic that bring the stage-business to life
by the simple device of giving Theseus and Lysander
a genial exchange of greetings, so that we can see the
latter bowing and smiling. Or consider the character of
Philostrate. Save for one line (5. 1. 106), the passage
quoted contains everything that he speaks in the play
—a matter of some twenty-two lines. Seven of these,
five belonging to one speech and two to another, are
irregularly arranged, and it is noteworthy that all seven
relate to some rehearsal of Quince's play at which
Philostrate professes to have been present. Now there
are two things to be said about this rehearsal: (i) that
according to the commentators, who know Shakespeare's
plays so much more exactly than he ever bothered to
know them himself, no such rehearsal can have taken
place, seeing that the one and only possible rehearsal
was performed in the wood, with Puck as the sole
'auditor'[1]; and (ii) that the account Philostrate gives us
of this impossible rehearsal and of his merriment thereat
—merriment which seems about to break forth afresh
in his suppressed chuckle, 'nothing, nothing in the
world'—provides us with the only human touch in his
portrait. The rehearsal, in short, was needed to endow
Philostrate with laughter, tears, and life; that 'his-
torically speaking' it can never have taken place mattered
neither to Shakespeare nor to his audience. Further—a
fascinating point—the italicised portions of Theseus'
opening speech are concerned with 'the poet'; in the
correctly arranged blank verse Theseus laughs, somewhat woodenly, at the 'seething brains' of lovers and
madmen, but says nothing about poets at all. In a word,

---

[1] v. Furness, *Variorum*, p. xxxiv.

'the poet' was an afterthought, inserted, like that sally
about players which Theseus utters later on in the scene
(ll. 210–11), with the object of quizzing the player-
poet's own craft. Finally, it is delightful to discover that
the gracious words—

> For never anything can be amiss,
> When simpleness and duty tender it—

come down to us with all the emphasis of a deliberate
insertion.

By this time the direction in which the facts are taking
us will be clear. The fifty-five regularly arranged lines
which stand by themselves were composed early—probably, if we are to judge from their style, very early in
Shakespeare's dramatic career: the eight patches of
irregularly arranged verse were added later, and being
written on the margin of the MS, in such space as could
be found, they presented a problem in line-arrangement
which the compositor was quite unable to solve. Furthermore, seeing that fifty-five lines represent about the
quantity of blank verse which Shakespeare probably
wrote to a page of foolscap[1], it is possible—we think,
even likely—that we are here dealing with the revision
of a single page of Shakespearian MS. We can, of
course, only guess at the length of the interval between
this revision and Shakespeare's first handling of the
page; but that it was a matter of years rather than of
hours or days is, we believe, suggested not merely by
the comparative maturity of style in the later material,
but also by the addition of 'the poet' in ll. 5–8, 12–17.
As a young man Shakespeare would, we may suppose,
take the muse too seriously to fling a jest at her, while

---

[1] v. *Shakespeare's Hand in the play of 'Sir Thomas More,'*
p. 116. It seems clear that Shakespeare was writing about
54 lines to a page in the MS of *2 Hen. IV.* Possibly he was
more economical of paper at the date of the first draft of
M.N.D. If so then the hypothetical page may have comprised ll. 1–88.

only a poet who rode easy in his seat and had triumphs behind him would be likely to kick up his heels so frankly as Shakespeare does in the glorious quip beginning 'The poet's eye, in a fine frenzy rolling.'

(ii) '*Puck*' *and the magic flower.*

Our excuse for dwelling thus long upon less than a hundred lines of the text must be that never again in the whole canon may we hope to catch so clear, so unquestionable, so happy a glimpse of Shakespeare at work upon his manuscript. Did he rehandle other pages at the same time as he made these additions to the beginning of what we now call the fifth act? We do not doubt it; and fortunately others share our view that *A Midsummer-Night's Dream* is a revised text. Mr E. K. Chambers, for example, a cautious critic, has picked out two passages, 3. 2. 177–344 and 5. 1. 1–105, as showing 'a markedly larger proportion' of feminine endings and mid-line pauses than the rest of the verse[1]. 'In the earlier passage,' he writes, 'this may be due merely to the excited state of the speakers, but I cannot resist the suspicion that the opening of Act 5 shows some traces of later work.' The bibliographical evidence brought forward above amply confirms his suspicions as to the opening of Act 5, while we shall in our notes show reasons for supposing that the conjectured revision in 3. 2. is at least highly probable, though the bibliographical clues are here less suggestive. But an earlier and far more whole-hearted believer in the revision than Mr Chambers was F. G. Fleay, who claimed to discover revision-clues throughout the text[2]. Some of these, which we shall deal with in our notes, seem to us either beside the point or of secondary importance. One, however, is of a very different order.

[1] v. pp. 14–15, 193, 195 of his edition of the play in the *Warwick Shakespeare.*
[2] *Life of Shakespeare* (1886), pp. 181–85.

We found both in *Much Ado* (v. pp. 95–7) and in *Love's Labour's Lost* (v. pp. 111–13) that Shakespeare, in revising a text, frequently changed the names or the titles of minor characters in stage-directions and speech-headings. Fleay's sharp eye noticed in the present text a curious alternation of the same kind between the names 'Puck' and 'Robin,' and he wrote: 'A careful examination has convinced me that wherever *Robin* occurs in the stage-directions or speech-prefixes scarcely any, if any, alteration has been made; *Puck*, on the contrary, indicates change.' Characteristically enough, he leaves it at that. He makes no attempt to explain the grounds of his conviction, or even to bring his bare assertion of it into connexion with another piece of dogmatism in which he declares that the play has a double ending, *Robin's* final speech being 'palpably a stage-epilogue [i.e. an epilogue written for the public theatre], while what precedes from *"Enter Puck"* to *"break of day. Exeunt"* is very appropriate for a marriage entertainment, but scarcely suited to the [public] stage.' In the circumstances, it is not surprising that his thesis has been either ignored or treated with contempt by later commentators, most of whom seriously underrate his critical acumen. But having ourselves received illumination from similar variations in other texts, we cannot put Fleay's theories aside without enquiry.

In the first place, most readers of the play would agree that 5. 1. 369–421 must have been written for a marriage entertainment in some private house (cf. note 5. 1. 389–90). The reference to 'the dead and drowsy fire,' at which the fairies were obviously intended to kindle tapers as they entered, the command to 'stray through this house' and bless 'each several chamber,' the mention of 'the best bride-bed,' 'the couples three,' and 'the owner,' who is clearly not one of the newly married persons, all point to a performance in the hall of some palace or nobleman's house in honour of a wedding, possibly a triple wedding. On the other hand, though Fleay's confident assertion that *Robin's* concluding lines (5. 1. 422–37) were 'palpably' penned for the public theatre was subsequently withdrawn[1], we have little doubt that these lines were written on a different occasion from that which gave us *Puck's* broom-speech and the fairy dance-song which follows it. The beautiful dismissal,

Trip away:
Make no stay:
Meet me all by break of day,

furnishes so perfect an ending to the play, with the stage growing darker and darker as the fairies dance out with their crowns of light[2], that we cannot believe anything was intended to come after, least of all this rather timorous plea for pardon from the audience, which ill accords with the happy self-confidence of Act 5 up to that point. Is it conceivable, for instance, that, having just given Theseus the jesting words 'No Epilogue, I pray you—for your play needs no excuse. Never excuse,' Shakespeare would tamely draw to an end by writing an apologetic epilogue of his own? When, therefore, we find that the Quarto, which reads '*Enter Pucke*' at l. 369 and heads the broom-speech *Puck* likewise, assigns the last sixteen lines of the play to *Robin*, we may be forgiven if we agree with Fleay that this epilogue belongs to an earlier stratum of the text than the fairy wedding-masque.

The *Robin-Puck* variation, however, is not only found in the finale of Act 5; it affects the whole play. Both names often occur, for no apparent reason, in the same scene, and the far-reaching character of the clue, if clue it be, is to be gauged by the fact that *Robin* has twenty

---

[1] v. his *Eng. Drama*, ii. 194, where he describes the epilogue as 'apparently for the court.'
[2] v. note 5. 1. 389–90.

speeches, amounting in all to just under a hundred lines, and *Puck* thirteen speeches, amounting to just over a hundred lines. A revision, therefore, which would account for the *Puck* speeches is likely to have been a drastic one, prompted, it would seem probable, by the necessity for structural alterations. If then we consider those parts of the text in which these *Puck* speeches or stage-directions are to be found, do we as a matter of fact come upon any grounds for supposing that structural alteration has taken place? Most clearly and unmistakably we do, and when the *Puck* passages are brought together even the motives for the alteration become apparent. Moreover, the discovery of these motives, one dramatic and the other theatrical, raises in turn questions of quite remarkable interest.

The *Puck* speech-headings first crop up, significantly enough, in the passage of all passages in the play which has attracted and baffled commentators most, namely 2. 1. 148–87, the famous lines concerning Cupid's assault upon an 'imperial votaress.' Apart from the question of the palpable allusion to the Queen, the dramatic purpose of these lines is clear: they describe the origin and character of the magic flower which causes all the complications that follow. Now every other reference in the play to the 'flower' or 'herb' or to its antidote (save one which can be readily accounted for in other ways) occurs either in a *Puck* speech or in close proximity with the word *Puck* in speech-heading or stage-direction, while on the other hand the only two *Puck* speeches which are not connected with the flower are the broomspeech in 5. 1., referred to above, and one at the beginning of 3. 2., where the prefix is probably due to some slight abridgment (cf. head-note 3. 2.). In other words, Fleay's clue leads us straight to the conclusion that the 'little western flower' was an afterthought on Shakespeare's part, that he substituted it for some other kind of charm, and that wherever the exact nature of the charm had been mentioned in the original text alteration was found necessary. What the first charm may have been we do not, of course, know; but that it was some sort of love-juice to be laid upon the eyes of sleeping persons can be seen from indirect allusions to it in the *Robin* passages (e.g. 3.2.35–40, 88–101, 448–52). Apparently, therefore, Shakespeare's primary purpose was to change the nature of the object from which the juice was extracted, though of course once he began rewriting a passage he tended to do more than was absolutely necessary. And if it be asked why he should go to all this trouble to effect an alteration of such seeming unimportance, the answer is that we cannot tell why until we know exactly what he meant by the 'little western flower.' If, for instance, as Mr Chambers appears to think[1], the reference to the flower was intended as a compliment to the bride for whose wedding the play was written or, as we prefer to put it, revised, then Shakespeare's trouble would be amply accounted for. Incidentally, such a compliment would fit in very neatly with the wedding-masque of 5. 1., which *ex hypothesi* was written at the same time.

But before discussing the question of a particular performance, let us look for a moment at a theatrical point connected with the *Puck* speech-headings. The text of the wedding-masque in 5. 1., heralded by 'Puck' with his broom, consists chiefly of an elaborate 'ditty' sung by a choir of fairies with Oberon as leader. Such a song, involving as it did the employment of a number of children with good voices, must have been very unusual in Shakespeare's theatre, as Mr Richmond Noble has pertinently reminded us recently[2]. It is likely enough, therefore, that Titania's lullaby at the beginning of 2. 2.,

[1] *The Occasion of 'A Midsummer-Night's Dream'* (pp. 154–60 in *The Book of Homage to Shakespeare*, 1916, ed. by Sir Israel Gollancz).

[2] *Shakespeare's Use of Song*, Richmond Noble, pp. 49–59.

which is also sung by a choir of fairies, was written at the same time. Now the episode (2. 2. 1–42) of which this song is part and which ends with Oberon's words as he squeezes the juice upon Titania's eyes, runs to just 33 lines in the Quarto. Obviously, however, Oberon's speech, or song, at the end of 2. 1., beginning 'I know a bank,' leads up to the bower-scene and should be taken with it. And if it be, we get 55 quarto lines or, in other words, the number of lines which, as we believe, Shakespeare normally wrote on a foolscap page. Have we then here, in 2. 1. 247 to 2. 2. 42, a page of Shakespearian manuscript, written on the same occasion as the song in 5. 1., and inserted into the prompt-book, in place of deleted matter? The suggestion, which on general grounds appears extremely probable, is converted into a practical certainty when we observe (i) that the Quarto begins the passage thus:

Haſt thou the flower there? Welcome wanderer.

Enter Pucke.

Puck. I, there it is;

and (ii) that this hypothetical page of supremely beautiful fairy dialogue and song is flanked by passages of dialogue between the lovers in what we regard as primitive Shakespearian verse. It is interesting to notice that the passage which precedes it (an altercation between Demetrius and Helena) itself runs to 59 lines, and is preceded in its turn by the *Puck* passage dealing with 'the imperial votaress' and the 'little western flower.' For our part, we think it not improbable that these 59 lines of lover-dialogue formed yet another page of manuscript in the prompt-book, written at a time when Shakespeare was a little more sparing of paper than he became later.

Few readers of the play will dispute that, if *A Midsummer-Night's Dream* be a text composed at different periods, the episodes concerning the lovers, episodes wherein the psychology is generally as crude as the verse is stiff and antithetical, are likely to belong to the earliest stratum. No doubt Shakespeare, in the course of revision, pruned them and added fresh touches here and there, as we shall suggest in our notes, or even, if Mr Chambers be correct in his surmise as to 3. 2. 177–344, occasionally rewrote passages of some length. But the bulk of these scenes undoubtedly belong to a very early period in Shakespeare's dramatic career. We arrive, then, at the general conclusion that there are at least two textual layers in *A Midsummer-Night's Dream*: one, represented chiefly by the dialogue of the lovers, which was written on the threshold of Shakespeare's career, and the other (including the allusion to Queen Elizabeth, 'I know a bank where the wild thyme blows,' 'You spotted snakes,' 'The lunatic, the lover, and the poet,' the concluding epithalamium, together with the majority of *Puck's* lines) which was written later, in honour of a wedding at some great nobleman's house. How many years separated these two handlings of the text? Was there any other revision besides that which can be traced in the *Puck* speech-headings? How are we to account for the Bottom scenes and the charming *Robin* fairy-scenes, e.g. the opening of 2. 1., and the latter half of 3. 1.? Can we assign approximate dates to the periods at which Shakespeare was at work upon the manuscript? It is to these and similar questions we must now turn.

(iii) *Allusions and occasions.*

Over and above the reference to the Queen, *A Midsummer-Night's Dream* contains at least three passages which are seemingly topical allusions. But as these passages suggest different dates, commentators on the look-out for *the* date and *the* occasion of the play have been somewhat baffled by them. Once however admit that the text has been subject to revision, and allusions pointing to different years become signposts instead of stumbling-blocks.

It will be convenient to begin by considering the famous passage in Philostrate's 'brief,' referring to

> The thrice three Muses mourning for the death
> Of learning, late deceased in beggary [5. 1. 52–3].

Since the days of Warburton this has been generally accepted as a reference of some kind to Spenser's *Teares of the Muses* (pub. 1591), and for long it was supposed that Spenser's own death in 1599 was indicated. In 1840, however, Knight advanced the more plausible theory that the words 'learning, late deceased in beggary' refer to the squalid death, on Sept. 3, 1592, of Robert Greene, dramatist and poet, who affected the title of 'utriusque Academiae in Artibus Magister' on his title-pages, and was constantly girding at the ignorance of poets more successful than himself. The dates of Greene's death and of the publication of *The Teares of the Muses* were sufficiently close to make such a combined allusion a happy one, while the glance at Spenser would be apt, seeing that Spenser's friend Gabriel Harvey had savagely attacked the memory of Greene almost before he was in his grave, and this attack, together with Nashe's reply and the lengthy controversy that ensued, provided entertainment for the reading public of London for some years. Nevertheless, Shakespeare, in giving Theseus the comment

> That is some satire, keen and critical,
> Not sorting with a nuptial ceremony,

was, we believe, thinking rather of himself than of Gabriel Harvey. For Greene on his death-bed had abused Shakespeare as an 'upstart crow,' and his words, printed in *A Groatsworth of Wit* (1592), also attracted some attention at the time, as is clear from Chettle's reference to them in another pamphlet of that year. No doubt Shakespeare's friends urged him to make

reply, and this we suggest was the form his reply took.
In the circumstances, it would be difficult to imagine a
retort at once more appropriate and effective. 'A satire,
keen and critical, upon the death of Robert Greene, M.A.'
Shakespeare seems to imply, 'would be easy to write,
but—the man is dead, and so enough.' In any event,
if we take the passage as an allusion to Greene's death,
the words 'late deceased' would point to its having been
written in the autumn of 1592 or the winter of 1592–3.
But the passage itself, it will be remembered, forms part
of that first draft of the opening page of 5. 1. which,
to judge by its style, must have been composed as early
as any part of the lovers' dialogue. In other words, we
believe that the reference to Greene's recent decease fixes
the date of Shakespeare's original handling of the play
as 1592 or earlier[1].

Whether Shakespeare at that time plotted the play
himself or merely worked over the drama of some other
playwright will perhaps never be ascertained. The only
presumably pre-Shakespearian play, known to us by
name, which might conceivably have formed the basis
of the *Dream*, is the mysterious *King of the Fairies*,
scornfully linked by both Nashe and Greene with another
drama called *Delfrigus* (unless this be a mere alternative
title for the same play), as part of the stock-in-trade of
a travelling company[2]. We have not, however, been
able to trace any clues to the existence of such a play
beneath the Shakespearian text, unless it be its curious
connexion, or seeming connexion, with old dramas like
Damon and Pythias, 1582 (v. note 5. 1. 335) and
Heywood's translation of Seneca's *Hercules Furens*,
1581 (v. note 1. 2. 27–34).

A second and undoubted topical allusion, first noticed
we believe by Malone, though strangely ignored by most

---

[1] It is of course possible that the Greene passage may have
been added in 1592 to a play written some years before.

[2] Cf. McKerrow, *Nashe*, iii. 324 and note.

modern critics except Fleay and Chambers, is to be
found in the elaborate precautions taken by Quince and
his company to avoid frightening the ladies with the
apparition of Master Snug-Lion (cf. 1. 2. 69–77; 3. 1.
25–42; 5. 1. 217–24). On August 30, 1594, while
King James and his queen sat at dinner on the occasion
of the baptism of Prince Henry of Scotland, a triumphal
car was drawn into the hall by a blackamoor. 'This
chariot,' we read, 'should have been drawne in by a
lyon, but because his presence might have brought some
feare to the nearest, or that the sights of the lights and
torches might have commoved his tameness, it was
thought meete that the Moor should supply that room[1].'
The incident seems to have caused no small amusement
in London, if we may judge from the use which Shakespeare makes of it in his play; for, in Mr Chambers'
words, 'it can hardly be doubted' that the lion-business
in the *Dream* 'is a reminiscence of what actually happened in the Scottish court[2].' And if all this be granted,
two important results follow as regards the textual history of the play: (i) that Shakespeare was revising his
Dream in the autumn of 1594 or winter of 1594–5,
while the joke about the Scots lion was still fresh in
men's memories, and (ii) that, since the allusion runs
like a thread throughout all the scenes in which the
mechanicals are prominent, presumably these scenes
took their present form on the occasion of the 1594–5
revision. That other scenes were worked over at the
same time is sufficiently proved by the existence of the
third allusion, the validity of which is strengthened by
its chiming in so exactly with the date of the lion incident.
We refer to the long passage in 2. 1., describing an
extraordinarily unseasonable summer, which, as most
critics agree, tallies precisely with records that have sur-
vived of an exceptionally wet and chilly summer in 1594

[1] Cf. Nichols, *Progresses of Elizabeth*, iii. 365.
[2] Chambers, *M.N.D.* (*Warwick Shakespeare*), p. 11.

(v. note 2. 1. 88–117). Furthermore, we assign most of the *Robin* speeches to the same revision. The delightful conversation, for instance, which *Robin* holds with a fairy at the beginning of 2. 1. falls between the first scene devoted to the mechanicals and the passage referring to the wet summer just spoken of, and we see no reason for supposing that this conversation was written at a different time from what precedes and follows it. Similarly 3. 1., which opens with the clowns in conclave and develops into a *Robin* fairy-scene, is obviously all of the same texture and was almost certainly, save perhaps for a touch here and there, entirely written in 1594. Our view, in a word, is that in 1594 Shakespeare revised not only the Bottom scenes but the fairy scenes as well, leaving however the lovers' scenes very much as they had been in the first draft. Moreover, we have a strong impression, based to some extent upon the absence of bibliographical disturbance in the Bottom scenes, that after the revision was completed in 1594 a fair copy of the whole text was undertaken, as it seems to have been with *Love's Labour's Lost* in 1593[1]. If we are correct in this surmise, all purely bibliographical anomalies in the Quarto of 1600 must be attributed to the latest handling of the text, which gave us the *Puck* speech-headings. And in point of fact, as we shall discover when we come to work out the textual analysis in our notes, this relegation of bibliographical irregularities to an occasion subsequent to 1594 answers very well. We

[1] v. p. 115 of our edition of *L.L.L.*, and head-note 2. 1. below. All bibliographical disturbances in the text being apparently later than 1594, it is very tempting to suppose that Shakespeare first handled the play in 1594 and only once revised it. We are, however, compelled to set aside this alluringly simple solution not only by the Greene allusion but also by the primitive character of the verse in the lover-dialogue, for which 1594 is, we feel, too late a date.

are not forgetting that up to the present 1594–5 has been the generally accepted date for the play as a whole. But it is, of course, obvious that if the *Robin* prefixes belong to 1594, the *Puck* revision, as we may call it, which we have already considered in some detail, must belong to a later date still. In other words, the fairy scenes, completely revised in 1594, were partially revised once again.

Shakespeare's final handling of the play gave us a topical allusion more elaborate than any of the three belonging to 1592 and 1594, namely Oberon's speech concerning 'the imperial votaress'; but this refers rather to the past than the present, and withal no one has yet discovered what it means. We have nothing, in short, in the *Puck* passages which will pin us down to a definite year for their composition. Nevertheless, there are several reasons why 1598 should be selected as a highly appropriate if not an absolutely certain date. The Fisher Quarto, printed in 1600, professes on its title-page to give the play 'as it hath beene sundry times publickely acted,' which suggests performances at the Globe sufficiently recent and public interest sufficiently alive for publication to have been worth Fisher's while. On the other hand, we can be certain that Fisher would never have secured the copyright from the Chamberlain's men unless they believed the play's acting possibilities to be exhausted for the time being. Supposing this belief forced upon them by dwindling receipts in the summers of 1599 and 1600, the play in its present form may have first appeared on the public stage in 1598. And this possibility falls in well with the fact that Meres mentions *A Midsummer-Night's Dream* in the famous list which occurs in his *Palladis Tamia*, entered in the Stationers' Register on Sept. 7, 1598.

The choric songs, again, which occur as we have seen in the latest sections of the text, indicate a date somewhere near 1598. Mr Richmond Noble, the only

critic who has seriously considered the songs of Shakespeare dramatically and theatrically, declares the fairy-
masque in 5. 1. to be 'a comparatively late addition,'
and writes: '*A Midsummer-Night's Dream* marks a very
important stage in Shakespeare's song career, and, if we
are to accept the very early date of 1595 as its first date
of presentation, one that causes very considerable difficulty in tracing that career. Shakespeare up till 1595
had had to resort to professional musicians, and even
later in 1597 in *Love's Labour's Lost* and 1 *Henry IV*,
he did not seem to be entirely unshackled in the matter.
Yet here in this play, right in the middle of these other
plays, he would appear to have suddenly at his disposal
plenty of children able both to sing and act[1].' Accordingly, following up a suggestion by Mr W. J. Lawrence[2],
he is inclined to date the play 1598 or thereabouts and
to associate it with *The Merry Wives*, 'in which there
are singing children' and which is usually assigned to
this year. The connexion with *The Merry Wives*, indeed,
is closer than Mr Noble himself realised. For not only
do both plays demand a choir of children who can sing
and act and dance; but in both the fairies wear crowns
of lighted tapers (v. note 5. 1. 389–90) and receive
instructions to bless a hallowed house. It would almost
seem, in fact, as if the success of the fairy-masque at the
original private performance of *A Midsummer-Night's
Dream* persuaded Shakespeare's company to introduce
the same device, or rather an inferior imitation of it, into
their hastily written and scantily rehearsed version of
The Merry Wives for the Court. At any rate the concluding acts of the two plays are twin productions from
the theatrical point of view, and only a short interval
of time can have separated the original performances.

[1] *Shakespeare's Use of Song*, p. 52.
[2] v. *Times Literary Supplement*, Dec. 9, 1920. Un-
fortunately Mr Lawrence does not, we feel, advance argu-
ments of any weight to support his thesis.

Furthermore, if *A Midsummer-Night's Dream*, as we now have it, was first put on the public stage in the summer of 1598, the original performance is likely to have taken place at some great wedding in the spring of that year. Was there any wedding about this time which would fit the circumstances?

It has, of course, long been recognised that *A Midsummer-Night's Dream* is a wedding-play, while its length—it runs to 2136 lines, and is the fourth shortest play in the canon—suggests that it was intended primarily for a private rather than a public performance. Accordingly various noble marriages have at different times been advanced as possible occasions for its production. For instance, the marriage of the Earl of Essex in 1590 to Frances, widow of Sir Philip Sidney, was proposed by Elze and supported by Kurz. This date is not now seriously entertained in any quarter, though, if parts of the text go back to some year before 1592, it cannot be dismissed as impossible. Curiously enough, no one, as far as we know, has quoted a wedding from 1592 or 1593 to fall in with the allusion to Robert Greene's death, and it may be that in his first draft Shakespeare had no particular wedding in view; certainly that draft did not contain the wedding-masque with which the transmitted text concludes. Nevertheless, even without the masque, the fable, as Dr Johnson would say, is so appropriate to a marriage-celebration, that it is hard to believe the play was not originally plotted to that end. And if so the revision of 1594 is likely to have been undertaken for a similar purpose. Now Jan. 26, 1595, the date of the marriage of William Stanley, Earl of Derby, to Elizabeth Vere, daughter of the Earl of Oxford, fits in very well with the 1594 allusions, and since Fleay first put it forward this match has been commonly regarded by critics as the most likely occasion for 'the composition of the play.' We have nothing better to offer for the revision of 1594, but we do not ourselves favour the Stanley wedding, since the Queen is reputed to have been present at it, and we very much doubt whether the *Dream*, in any form, can have been played before her[1].

Finally, there is the marriage of the Earl of Southampton in 1598 to Elizabeth Vernon, cousin and protégée of the Earl of Essex, an occasion which, first suggested a little half-heartedly by Tieck, and subsequently taken up more fervently by Gerald Massey, has of late found few supporters. Indeed an apparently insuperable obstacle has hitherto stood in the way of its acceptance, namely the patent absurdity, as it would seem to anyone in the least acquainted with the development of Shakespeare's powers and style, of supposing that he could be writing this play, *as a whole*, so late as the year 1598. But this obstacle vanishes directly the fact of revision be admitted. It seems to us, therefore, at least possible that Shakespeare undertook the last revision, to which we owe nearly all the finest poetry of the play, in celebration of his friend and patron's marriage, and that the 'little western flower' of which Oberon speaks was none other than Elizabeth Vernon, daughter of Sir John Vernon of Hodnet Hall, Shropshire. This suggestion, we should add, is attended with certain chronological difficulties, which cannot be gone into here. We will only say that we do not regard them as fatal to the possibility. In any event, the evidence brought forward in the preceding paragraphs should suffice, we hope, to establish a presumption in favour of *A Midsummer-Night's Dream* having been first handled by Shakespeare in 1592 or before, rehandled in 1594, and rehandled once again in 1598. The test of such a hypothesis is the way in which it works out in detail. We shall bring it to this test in the notes that follow.

D. W.

[1] Cf. *Title-page of the Quarto*, p. 101, *Characters in the Play* (Titania), p. 103, and notes 1. 1. 72–8; 2. 1. 148–87; 3. 1. 145–46.

NOTES

All significant departures from the Quarto are recorded; the name of the critic who first suggested the new reading being given in brackets. Illustrative spellings and misprints are quoted from the Good Quartos or from the Folio where no Good Quarto exists. The line-numeration for reference to plays not yet issued in this edition is that of Bartlett's *Concordance*.

Q. stands for the Quarto of 1600 (Fisher); Q. 1619 for the faked Jaggard Quarto, v. p. 77; F., unless otherwise specified for the First Folio; T.I. = the Textual Introduction to be found in the *Tempest* volume; Sh. Hand = *Shakespeare's Hand in the play of 'Sir Thomas More'* (Camb. Univ. Press, 1923); Chambers = *M. N. D.* ed. by E. K. Chambers (The Warwick Shakespeare); Fleay = *The Life of Shakespeare* by F. G. Fleay; N.E.D. = *The New English Dictionary*; Sh. Eng. = *Shakespeare's England*; S.D. = stage-direction; G. = Glossary.

Title-page of the Quarto. For 'as it hath beene sundry times publickely acted' v. p. 97; for the imprint v. pp. 78–9. In view of the common assumption by edd. that *M. N. D.* was played before Queen Elizabeth, it is noteworthy that no such claim is made upon the title-page.

Characters in the Play. Neither Q. nor F. contains a list of the Names of all the Actors, and the 'Dramatis personae' were first supplied by Rowe. We have thought it convenient to separate the court, the mechanicals and the fairies—a departure from our usual custom. The character-names in this play demand special attention:

(i) The Court. The names *Theseus, Hippolyta, Egeus, Demetrius, Lysander*, seem to be derived, almost haphazardly, from North's 'Plutarch.' Theseus, 'Duke of Athens' and husband of the 'bouncing Amazon' Hippolyta, is of course the King Theseus of legend, to whom Plutarch devotes a 'life'; and from this 'Life of Theseus' a number of references in the play are evidently taken (v. note 2. 1. 78–80). On the other hand, Egeus is the father of Theseus in Plutarch's account, while Demetrius and Lysander are just names which happen to occur elsewhere in North's volume. The name *Philostrate* comes from the other chief source for this play, Chaucer's 'Knight's Tale,' being the pseudonym taken by Arcite when he served in disguise at the court of Theseus. (ii) The Mechanicals. Commentators have remarked that *Bottom* takes his name from the 'bottom' or core of the skein upon which the weaver's yarn is wound; but they have not noticed that most of the other clowns have technical names likewise. Thus *Quince* is simply a spelling of 'quines' or 'quoins,' i.e. wedge-shaped blocks of wood used for building purposes, and therefore appropriately connected with a carpenter; *Snout* means nozzle or spout (v. N.E.D. 'snout' 4), which suggests the tinker's trade in mending kettles; *Snug* means 'compact, close-fitting, tight'—a good name for a joiner; and *Flute*, the bellows-mender, would of course have to repair fluted church-organs as well as the domestic bellows. *Starveling*, indeed, is the only non-technical name among them, though it is apt enough, alluding as it does to the proverbial leanness of tailors, of whom it took 'nine to make a man[1].' (iii) The Fairies. *Oberon* is the name of the King of Faery in 'Huon of Bordeaux'; Spenser also refers to him in 'The Faerie Queene' (ii. 1. 6; ii. 10. 75), where he is made

---

[1] Cf. 'Francis Feeble' the woman's tailor in 2 *Hen. IV*, 3. 2. 158–72.

out to be the father of Gloriana (in other words Henry
VIII). *Titania* seems to be Shakespeare's own name
for the Fairy Queen. He found it in the original Ovid's
'Metamorphoses'—it does not occur in Golding's
translation—where it is used as a title for Diana. No one
has apparently observed hitherto that Shakespeare may
have run some risk in giving one of Diana's titles to his
Fairy Queen, seeing that Diana and Fairy Queen were
names commonly bestowed upon Queen Elizabeth herself (cf. notes 1. 1. 72–8; 2. 1. 123, 148–87). *Robin
Goodfellow* is a name; *Puck* is strictly speaking a title for
a class of mischievous or malicious sprites, and it is
noticeable that Robin is never addressed simply as
'Puck' in the text, though 'my gentle Puck' and 'sweet
Puck' occur. The names 'Puck' and 'Robin' occur
indiscriminately in the Quarto speech-headings and
S.D.s; for the significance of this v. pp. 86–92. For
Moth v. G. and note 3. 1. 166–69.

Acts and Scenes. No divisions in Q. The F. divides
into acts only, which divisions, though followed in all
mod. editions, are patently absurd and were clearly introduced into the text after Shakespeare had left the Globe,
probably after his death. Cf. p. 158 and T.I. § 3.

Punctuation. The punctuation of this text is only
moderately good, v. p. 79. We have treated most of
the periods of the original as if they were commas.
On the other hand all Q. colons and semi-colons
have been carefully considered and none have been
rejected without record in the notes, save a few
which have been translated as notes of exclamation.
Dots have only been used where the Q. prints semi-
colons or periods, while the introduction of fresh colons
or semi-colons has always been noted.

Stage-directions. All original S.D.s are given in the
notes, according to Q., where Q. and F. are in substantial agreement. The F. S.D.s (for which v. pp. 154–
59) are also quoted where they differ from those of Q.

1. 1.

The material, we conjecture, of this scene is mainly from the first draft, though it was probably copied out and perhaps adapted in 1594. Fleay believed it to be composed of two original scenes spliced together, which seems to us plausible (v. note ll. 128–251). Possibly, also, the opening nineteen lines were first written in 1594; and possibly Shakespeare had some special reason at that time for introducing the reference to 'four days' (v. note ll. 2–3) which conflicts with the time-analysis elsewhere in the play. If so, the addition may have been needed in order to introduce Hippolyta into the scene. Cf. notes ll. 123–26 below and 4. 1. head-note. We suggest that ll. 143–49 (v. note l. 142) may have been added in 1598.

S.D. Q. 'Enter Theseus, Hippolita, with others.' For our setting of the scene cf. head-note S.D. 5. 1.

1–19. These lines evidently owe a good deal to the opening passage of Chaucer's *Knightes Tale*.

2–3. *four happy days...Another moon* i.e. four days must pass before the wedding-day. Yet the lovers arrange in this same scene to meet in the wood 'to-morrow night,' and the very next morning after this meeting we find Theseus, Hippolyta and the other couples repairing to the temple for the marriage. The discrepancy is probably due to alterations in the course of revision. Cf. head-note. For the problem of the moon, which troubles many, v. note 3. 1. 50–3.

4. *wanes* (Q. 1619) Q. 'waues'

5. *dowager* v. G.

7. *night* (Q.) Q. 1619 'nights', followed by F. and many mod. edd.

10. *New-bent* (Rowe) Q. 'Now bent'—an *o:e* misprint. Cf. T.I. p. xlii and Sh. Hand, p. 119.

15. *companion* v. G. Q. gives no 'exit' for Philostrate.

19. S.D. Q. 'Enter Egeus and his daughter Hermia,
and Lyſander, and Helena, and Demetrius.' (i) The
vain repetition of 'and' in the S.D.s is a characteristic
of this text (cf. head-notes 1. 2.; 4. 1. and 5. 1. 125
S.D.). A single duplication might suggest revision (cf.
Ado, p. 94), but this superfluity of 'ands' must be put
down to the compositor, perhaps expanding a carelessly
framed S.D. in his 'copy.' (ii) F. cut out Helena from
this S.D. and all edd. have followed suit. She has nothing
to say before l. 181 where Q. gives her a second entry;
but her entry here with the other lovers may have been
necessary in the original draft.

24. *Stand forth, Demetrius* 26. *Stand forth, Lysander*
Q. prints these in italics as stage-directions. They were
probably written as separate half-lines in the original
MS, to denote deliberate utterance (cf. *Measure*, note
2. 2. 83–4), and thus led the compositor astray. The
error was first rectified by Rowe.

27. *witched* (Theobald) Q. 'bewitched' F2 reads
'This hath bewitched' The compositors of this Q. took
scant heed of elisions; v. p. 79.

31. *love:* Q. 'loue,' 32. *fantasy* Q. 'phantaſie:'—
transposed pointing.

32. *And stol'n* etc. 'And imprinted thyself by stealth
upon her fancy' (E. K. Chambers).

45. *Immediately* v. G.

54. *in this kind* i.e. as a husband.

69. *Whether* Probably Shakespeare wrote 'whe'er'
and the compositor has filled out the original elision. v.
p. 79, and cf. *Temp.* 5. 1. 111 and *Errors*, 4. 1. 60.

72–8. *To live a barren sister...single blessedness*
These are remarkable lines; evidently written with
Queen Elizabeth in mind. But phrases like 'barren
sister' and 'withering on the virgin thorn' would surely
have sounded harsh in her ears. Cf. note 2. 1. 148–87.

74. *their blood* Q. 'there bloode'

99. *well derived* v. G.

123–26. Demetrius and Egeus...concerns yourselves
It is noteworthy that this is a repetition, in other words,
of ll. 114–16 above. Possibly it was added at the time
of the 1594 revision together with l. 122. N.B. (i) If
ll. 1–19 be also a 1594 addition, it looks as though
Hippolyta did not appear in this scene at all in the
original draft. Cf. head-note 4. 1. and note 4. 1. 185.
(ii) We are here just at the junction between Fleay's
two conjectured scenes. v. next note but one.

127. S.D. Q. 'Exeunt.' F. adds 'Manet Lyſander
and Hermia.'

128–251. This section, writes Fleay (*Life*, p. 185),
'ought to form, and probably did in the original play,
a separate scene; it certainly does not take place in the
palace.' Upon this Chambers comments 'The interview
between the lovers...is carefully led up to in what
precedes. Theseus' commands to Egeus and Demetrius
to accompany him have no significance in the story: they
are only the playwright's rather crude device to clear the
stage for Lysander and Hermia. Moreover...the F. stage-
direction disposes of Fleay's view.' Mr Chambers mis-
takes Fleay's argument, which is that the two sections
were separate scenes in the original draft of the play but
had been fused (by 'the playwright's rather crude device') in the course of revision. In any event the F.
S.D. has nothing to do with the question. On the other
hand, Fleay's contention that the lovers' conversation
could not have 'taken place in the palace' counts for
very little, seeing that it is mere surmise that the opening episodes of 1. 1. took place in a palace at all. Aldis
Wright's comment, 'It was a strange oversight on the
part of Egeus to leave his daughter with Lysander,' is
much more to the point. N.B. Q. reads 'Exeunt' at
l. 127 which suggests the end of a scene: F. adds 'Manet
Lyſander and Hermia' by way of showing that the scene
continues.

133. *hear* Q. 'here'

135, 137, 139. Q. ends each of these lines with a semi-colon.

136. *low* (Theobald)　Q. 'loue'—an emendation accepted by all edd.

142. *siege to it*—　Q. 'ſiege to it;' This semi-colon, which is out of place here, corresponds with the three Q. semi-colons (ll. 135, 137, 139) that mark the interruption of Lysander's speech by Hermia's exclamations. May it not be that it likewise, once, stood at the end of a speech, which was followed directly by Hermia's 'If then true lovers' etc. (l. 150)? If so then ll. 143–49, the splendour of which has been acclaimed by every editor of the play, were a marginal addition made in revision. That the verse-lining of this passage is correct may be explained on the supposition that it was either inserted into the fair-copy of 1594 (v. p. 96) or written in 1598 at right angles to the original column of verse (there might be room in the margin for seven lines thus written, cf. *L.L.L.* note 2. 1. 13). The contrast between the strength, beauty and swiftness of this passage and the insipidity of what follows is very striking; we are inclined to attribute it to 1598.

143. *momentany* v. G.　　　146. *spleen* v. G.

151. *It stands as an edict in destiny* A very poor line of verse, which we take to be a piece of patchwork designed to cover a rent in the text. The clumsy duplication of 'then' in ll. 150 and 152 strongly suggests a 'cut,' possibly of some half-dozen lines to balance the insertion of ll. 143–49.

152. *patience,* Q. 'patience:'　　155. *Fancy* v. G.

171. *simplicity...doves* v. G. 'simplicity.'

179. S.D. Q. 'Enter Helena.' Cf. note l. 19 above.

187. *Yours would I* (Hanmer)　Q. 'Your words I' The emendation is accepted by practically all mod. edd. Cf. 'wood' misprinted 'word' *L.L.L.* 4. 3. 244.

191. *I'ld* (Clark and Wright) Q. 'ile'—*e:d* misprint. Cf. T.I. p. xli and Sh. Hand, p. 119.

translated = transformed. Cf. Quince's use of the same word at 3. 1. 114.

192. *art* v. G.   205. *to me:* Q. 'to me.'

216. *sweet* (Theobald) Q. 'sweld'—an *e:d* misprint of 'swete,' a common 16th c. sp. Cf. T.I. p. xli and Sh. Hand, p. 119.

219. *stranger companies* (Theobald) Q. 'strange companions' The misprint would be partly explained if Shakespeare wrote 'companies' in such a way that it looked like 'companiõs.' The rhyme makes Theobald's emendation certain.

223. S.D. Q. 'Exit Hermia.'
225. S.D. Q. 'Exit Lyſander.'
230. *eyes*, Q. 'eyes:'
245. *dissolved* v. G. 'dissolve.'
249. *a dear expense* i.e. 'it will cost me dear, because it will be in return for my procuring him a sight of my rival' (Aldis Wright).   251. S.D. Q. 'Exit.'

1. 2.

We assign this scene to 1594 (v. pp. 95–6) though presumably another form of it existed previously.

S.D. Q. 'Enter Quince, the Carpenter; and Snugge, the Ioyner; and Bottom, the Weauer; and Flute, the Bellowes mender; & Snout, the Tinker; and Starueling, the Tayler.' F. following Q. 1619 omits all but the last 'and.' For the character-names v. p. 102 and for the repetition of 'and' cf. note 1. 1. 19.

2. *generally* Bottom of course means 'severally.'

8. *Peter Quince* Q. 'Peeter Quince' This spelling of 'Peter' occurs six times in present text, but not apparently elsewhere in the canon. It is perhaps a compositor's idiosyncrasy.

10. *grow to a point* v. G.

11–12. *The most lamentable comedy* Shakespeare was fond of laughing at the conventional classification of drama. Cf. Polonius' famous list (*Ham.* 2. 2. 415–20).

Probably the playbills of the age provided him with occasions for such laughter; or the title-pages of his own quartos may even have done so, if he ever saw them, e.g. 'The most excellent and lamentable Tragedie of Romeo and Iuliet,' 'The comicall History of the Merchant of Venice,' etc.

12. *Pyramus and Thisby.* The story is found in Golding's 'Ovid' (iv. 55–166). Other versions were available in Chaucer's *Legend of Good Women* and in a contemporary ballad entitled 'A New Sonet of Pyramus and Thisbe' by one I.Thomson (1584). 'Thisbe' is of course the classical form: we use the spelling which is alone found in the Q. and was undoubtedly Shakespeare's.

25. *Ercles* v. note ll. 27–34 below. Hercules was a stock figure on the stage, like Termagent or Herod; cf. Greene's *Groatsworth of Wit* (1592), 'The twelve labours of Hercules have I terribly thundered on the stage,' and (with the whole passage) *Ham.* 3. 2. 9–17 'O, it offends me to the soul to hear a robustious periwig-pated fellow tear a passion to tatters, to the very rags, to split the ears of the groundlings...it out-herods Herod.'

25–6. *to tear a cat in, to make all split* proverbial expressions for stage-ranting. v. G. 'tear a cat,' 'split.'

26. *split.* Q. 'fplit'   27. *rocks* Q. 'rocks:'

27–34. Q. prints these lines as prose. Rolfe quotes from Jasper Heywood's translation of Seneca's *Hercules Furens* (1581):

> O Lord of ghosts! whose fiery flash
>   That forth thy hand doth shake,
> Doth cause the trembling lodges twain
>   Of Phœbus' car to shake.

*   *   *   *

> The roaring rocks have quaking stirr'd,
>   And none thereat hath push'd;
> Hell gloomy gates I have brast ope
>   Where grisly ghosts all hush'd
> Have stood...

That there is some connexion between these lines and Bottom's looks very possible; yet there seems no reason why Shakespeare should burlesque a translation ten or a dozen years old. Perhaps the text here goes back to some pre-Shakespearian version. v. p. 94.

41. *What is Thisby* etc. Q. heads this *Fla.* for *Flu.*

48. *thisne, thisne*— Q. 'Thiſne, Thiſne,' Q. prints the word in italics and with a capital letter, which shows that the compositor took it for a name; and all edd. have followed suit. Clark and Wright, however, question 'whether the true reading is not "thisne, thisne"; that is, "in this manner," a meaning which "thissen" has in several dialects.' We believe this is what Shakespeare intended, for the simple reason, which appears to have escaped the notice of all, that it would be absurd (even for Bottom) to call out Thisby's name when he is pretending to be Thisby herself. It is also to be remarked that 'thisne' ends with an *e* while 'Thisby' is always spelt with a *y* in the Q.

55–8. *Thisby's mother...Pyramus' father...Thisby's father* There were dramatic possibilities in these characters, seeing that it was the 'wrecched jelous fadres,' as Chaucer calls them (*The Legend of Thisbe of Babylon*), quite as much as 'Wall, that vile Wall,' which did the lovers sunder, and possibly they figured more prominently in the first draft. After assigning the parts, however, in 1594 Shakespeare makes no further use of them, either in the rehearsal or the play itself. Cf. note 3. 1. 76–98.

67. *say,* Q. 'ſay;'

70–1. *fright the duchess and the ladies...hang us all.* Cf. pp. 95–6. This passage fixes the date of the present version of the scene as later than August 30, 1594.

85–8. *straw-colour...perfect yellow* Bottom, the weaver, rattles off the names of various dyes familiar to him in his craft: for 'purple-in-grain' cf. Cotgrave (1611), 'grain, wherewith cloth is dyed in grain.'

94. *a mile without the town* a careless echo of 'a league without the town' (1. 1. 165).

100. *obscenely* v. G.

103. *hold, or cut bow-strings* v. G. S.D. Q. 'Exeunt.'

2. 1.

According to the conjectural analysis given in outline on pp. 86–92 this scene falls into four sections: (i) ll. 1–147 written in 1594. Note the delightful fairy-dialogue, with *Robin* speech-headings, and the description of the disastrous summer of 1594. (ii) ll. 148–187 written in 1598. Note *Puck* speech-headings and the introduction of the 'little western flower' motive. (iii) ll. 188–246, early Shakespearian verse—probably a MS page (= 59 ll.) from the original draft. (iv) ll. 247–68 written in 1598; bibliographically to be considered with the opening of 2. 2. (v. head-note 2. 2.)

S.D. Q. 'Enter a Fairie at one doore, and Robin goodfellow at another.' Clearly a prompt-book S.D. Cf. p. 80. For our setting v. head-note S.D. 2. 2.

1. *How now, spirit* etc. Q. heads this speech *Robin* and so with all Puck's speeches down to l. 59.

7. *moonës* (Steevens) Q. 'Moons' The line is crowded in Q. and the compositor would have every inducement to omit the *e*. For 'sphere' v. G.

9. *To dew her orbs* Cf. *Temp.* 5. 1. 36–8.

10. *pensioners* v. G.

15. *And hang a pearl* etc. Imitated in *The Wisdom of Doctor Doddypoll*, an anonymous play first printed in 1600, act 3, sc. 5:

'Twas I that led you through the painted meads,
Where the light fairies danced upon the flowers,
Hanging on every leaf an orient pearl.

Fleay wrongly assumes that because Nashe refers to Doctor Doddypoll in 1596 the play must be earlier than this date. We find 'Doctor Doddypoll' used as a term of abuse as early as 1581 (v. N.E.D. 'doddypoll').

16. *lob of spirits* v. G. 'lob.'

20. *wrath*, Q. 'wrath:'

26. *withholds* Q. 'withhoulds' Cf. note 5. 1. 370.

35. *villagery* Q. 'Villageree'

36–8. *Skim milk...no barm* Cf. 'Your grandam's maids were wont to set a bowl of milk before...Robin Goodfellow, for grinding of malt or mustard and sweeping the house at midnight' (Reginald Scot, *Discovery of Witchcraft*, bk iv. ch. x.).

42–3. Q. prints 'Thou speakeſt aright...the night' in one line. This and the fact that l. 42 is short suggest some slight abridgment or adaptation of the text.

45. *beguile*, Q. 'beguile;' 46. *foal;* Q. 'fole,'— transposed pointing.

50. *dewlap* Q. 'dewlop'—a Shakespearian spelling.

54. *'tailor' cries* v. G. 'tailor.'

54–5. *cough...loff* Q. 'coffe...loffe' The spelling 'coffe' occurs in *Oth.* 4. 2. 29; *Troil.* 1. 3. 173; *Rom.* 3. 1. 28; cf. also 'coffing' *L.L.L.* 5. 2. 918; but 'loffe' (= laugh) is apparently not found elsewhere in Shakespeare, though common in the 16th cent. Cf. *Temp.* 2. 1. 185 (note). We retain 'loff' for the sake of the rhyme.

55. *hold* Q. 'hould' Cf. note 5. 1. 370.

58. *faëry* (Staunton: Johnson conj.) Q. 'Faery' The fact that Q. never uses this spelling elsewhere is strong evidence that Shakespeare intended the trisyllabic pronunciation here.

59. S.D. Q. 'Enter the King of Fairies, at one doore, with his traine; and the Queene, at another, with hers.' Another obvious prompt-book S.D. v. p. 80.

61. *Fairies, skip* (Theobald) Q. 'Fairy ſkippe'

66–8. *Corin...Phillida* v. G. 'Corin.'

69. *steep* (Q. 1619) Q. 'ſteppe' (< step) The spelling 'step' (=steppe) for 'steep' occurs in *Ham.* 1. 3. 48. The word 'steppe' in the modern sense, which is of course

connected with Russia and not with India, seems to have
been quite unknown in Shakespeare's day. Cf. *Comus*
140 'on the Indian steep' and v. N.E.D. 'steep' B 1.

70. *the bouncing Amazon* Hippolyta was, of course,
queen of the Amazons.

78–80. *Perigouna … Ægles … Ariadne … Antiopa.*
Shakespeare took these names from the 'Life of Theseus'
in North's 'Plutarch,' as will be clear from the following
extracts quoted from vol. i. of G. H. Wyndham's ed.
in the 'Tudor Translations':

This Sinnis had a goodly fair daughter called Perigouna,
which fled away, when she saw her father slain....But
Theseus finding her, called her, and sware by his faith he
would use her gently, and do her no hurt, nor displeasure
at all. Upon which promise she came out of the bush, and
lay with him, by whom she was conceived of a goodly boy
(p. 36).

After he was arrived in Creta, he slew there the Minotaur
(as the most part of ancient authors do write) by the means
and help of Ariadne....Some say that Ariadne hung herself
for sorrow, when she saw that Theseus had cast her off.
Others write, that she was transported by mariners into the
Isle of Naxos...and they think Theseus left her, because he
was in love with another, as by these verses should appear:

> Ægles, the Nymph, was loved of Theseus,
> Which was the daughter of Panopeus...

Other hold opinion, that Ariadne had two children by
Theseus (pp. 45–7).

Touching the voyage he made by the sea Major, Philo-
chorus and some other hold opinion that he went thither
with Hercules against the Amazons: and that to honour his
valiantness, Hercules gave him Antiopa, the Amazon....But
Clidemus the historiographer...calleth the Amazon which
Theseus married, Hippolyta, and not Antiopa (pp. 55–7).

78. *Perigouna* (Grant White) Q. 'Perigenia'—a
combined minim and *o:e* misprint. (Cf. T.I. pp. xli–
xlii.) For 'Perigouna' see previous note. The Q. error
is so much in the run of the ordinary misprints in the
Qq. that it is almost certainly due to the compositor

rather than to careless transcription by Shakespeare from North. As Cunningham ('Arden' edition) remarks, 'Shakespeare had nothing to gain, either in rhythm or otherwise, by altering the spelling.'

79. *Ægles* (Chambers) Q. 'Eagles' All edd. but Chambers and Cunningham read Ægle, the correct classical form: but Shakespeare found 'Aegles' in North (v. note ll. 78–80) and the Q. 'Eagles' proves he followed it.

82. *the middle summer's spring* i.e. the beginning of midsummer. v. G. 'spring.'

85–6. *Or in the beachèd margent* etc. Cf. *Temp.* 1. 2. 376–80; 5. 1. 34–6.

88–117. *Therefore the winds* etc. This passage was almost certainly written after the extraordinarily bad summer of 1594. Cf. pp. 95–6. The contemporary allusions to the weather at this period are too many and too long to quote: the shortest and most apt comes from the preface to Churchyard's *Charity* (1595): 'A great nobleman told me this last wet summer, the weather was too cold for poets.'

91. *Hath* So Q. Most edd. follow Rowe and read 'Have'

97. *murrion* v. G.

98. *nine men's morris* v. G.   99. *mazes* v. G.

101. *want their winter here* Edd. have uniformly condemned 'here' as corrupt, but have not agreed upon a substitute. In our judgment, far the best suggestion out of a large number is Brae's *gear*. The confusion of 'gere' and 'here' is not at all impossible in English script, and Shakespeare formed both *g* and *h* with sickle-like terminations very similar in appearance (v. Sh. Hand, Plate v). Moreover 'gear' (= clothes) fits the context excellently. 'The summer is so cold,' says Titania in effect, 'that the humans need their winter clothes'; and she develops this idea of coldness in the next line, which refers, not to Christmas carols as many

commentators seem to have imagined, but to the songs
and dances of May-time or the summer 'wakes,' semi-
religious merry-makings that lasted all night. Cf. 'wake'
L.L.L. G., and P. Stubbes' description of 'May-games,'
Anatomie of Abuses (ed. Furnivall, i. 149). 'Carole,'
writes Chambers, 'seems to become a term for popular
rejoicing in general' (*Mediaeval Stage*, i. 164).

104. *air,* Q. 'aire;' 105. *abound:* Q. 'abound'—
transposed pointing.

106–14. *And thorough this distemperature...which
is which* It is to be noted that in these lines Titania is no
longer describing the bad summer, but speaks of a general
confusion of the seasons. Possibly the whole passage was
written late in 1594 when the wet summer had been
followed by a mild winter.

109. *thin* (Tyrwhitt) Q. 'chinne' For *t:c* misprints
cf. *L.L.L.* note 5. 1. 116. The error was particularly
likely to happen before *h*; but in any case Shakespeare's
t and *c* were often dangerously alike (cf. Sh. Hand,
Plates v and vi).

115–16. *evils comes/From our* Q. divides 'euils,/
Comes from our'

120. *a little changeling boy* Cf. 'stol'n from an
Indian king' l. 22 above. It has been supposed by most
commentators that the account which Titania now gives
of the boy's birth (ll. 123–37) conflicts with the 'changeling' story. On the contrary, it develops it. The mother,
concubine of an Indian king, dies in child-bed; and
Titania, for love of the mother, steals the child. Conceivably this 'changeling' story may have been more
prominent in the version of 1594 or of 1592.

123. *a vot'ress of my order* If Titania be Diana (cf.
p. 103) it is remarkable that this mother should be a
'vot'ress' of her 'order.'

135. *die;* Q. 'dye,' 136. *boy,* Q. 'boy;'—transposed pointing.

145. S.D. Q. 'Exeunt.'

148–87. *My gentle Puck*, etc. The two brief speeches of Puck in this famous passage are headed *Puck* and *Pu.* respectively by Q. v. head-note and pp. 87–92. Furness devotes sixteen and a half pages of notes in his *Variorum Shakespeare* to these forty lines, which contain of course an allusion to Queen Elizabeth, to some 'entertainment' provided for her by one of her suitors, and, presumably, to another lady designated as 'a little western flower.' Beyond that, all is in dispute. It is, we think, unnecessary here to reproduce the conflicting theories of commentators, still less to advance a fresh one of our own. All we would say is that we are not convinced that the lines would have been taken as complimentary by the Queen had she heard them spoken from the stage, as has been commonly assumed. Surely the oblation of flattery is scanty—the Vestal is 'fair,' that is all—while even maiden ladies of ordinary rank are apt to be touchy about references to past courtships. Worst of all, the 'little western flower' so obviously gets the best of it! In short, we doubt very much whether Elizabeth was ever present at this play at all. Cf. pp. 101, 103 and notes 1. 1. 72–8; 3. 1. 145–46.

158. *the west* (F.) Q. 'weft'

168. *Love-in-idleness* v. G.

175–76. *I'll put...forty minutes* Q. prints in one line, and gives no 'exit' for Puck.

183. *from off* Q. 'from of'—a Shakespearian spelling.

184. *another herb* i.e. 'Dian's bud,' cf. 4. 1. 72.

186. *I am invisible* This hint to the audience, not of course to Puck, is a little crude, but would be natural enough if Shakespeare were revising, and stitching, so to speak, a new piece on to an old text, as we believe he was here. Cf. head-note and p. 91.

187. S.D. Q. 'Enter Demetrius, Helena following him.'

190. *slay...slayeth* (Theobald) Q. 'ftay...ftayeth'

192. *wood*, Q. 'wood:' 193. *Hermia:* Q. 'Hermia.'
—transposed pointing.

194. *get thee* Q. 'get the'—a Shakespearian spelling,
frequent in the Qq.

196. *But yet you draw not iron* i.e. but yet you do not
draw your sword to slay me. The point of the passage
seems to have been hitherto missed because no one has
suspected a quibble. Cf. l. 190 above. Shakespeare
constantly uses 'iron' for 'sword,' e.g. *Troil.* 2. 3. 18
'drawing their massy irons.'

iron, for (F.) Q. 'Iron. For'

201. *not nor* (F.) Q. 'not, not'

203. *I am your spaniel* etc. Cf. *Two Gent.* 4. 2. 14–15
'Yet, spaniel-like, the more she spurns my love,/The
more it grows, and fawneth on her still.'

206. *lose* (F.) Q. 'loofe' Shakespeare made no
difference in the spelling of these two words, and loves
to quibble upon them (cf. *L.L.L.* notes 4. 3. 71, 358).
After 'spaniel' ll. 203, 205, a quibble is probably
intended here.

220. *privilege: for that* Q. 'priuiledge: For that'
Malone and many mod. edd. read 'privilege for that;'
The Q. reading gives good sense, and we ought not
lightly to throw over a colon and a capital.

237, 244. Q. gives no 'exits' for Demetrius and
Helena—possibly an indication that the text has been
disturbed.

246. S.D. Q. 'Enter Pucke.' Cf. 2. 2. head-note
and p. 91.

249. *I know a bank* etc. The prosodists cavil at this
line, which is awkward to scan and has only nine
syllables. Yet no ear can refuse to accept it as verse and
very delightful verse. Surely the explanation is that
ll. 249–58 were intended to be sung and that Shakespeare had a particular air in mind as he composed
them. But cf. Noble, *Shakespeare's Use of Song*, pp. 54–5.

268. S.D. Q. 'Exeunt.'

2. 2.

The present scene falls textually into four divisions:
(i) ll. 1–42 (= 33 Q. lines). This section taken with the
last 22 lines of 2. 1., gives us, as we believe, a page of
Shakespearian MS, added in 1598 (v. pp. 90–91). It
can hardly be doubted, in any event, that Shakespeare
wrote the whole passage under the same poetic impulse
and probably at a single sitting; (ii) ll. 43–73, which
we take to be first draft; (iii) ll. 74–91, a short-lined
trochaic passage, dealing with the 'flower's force in
stirring love,' assigned to *Puck*, and headed 'Enter
Pucke' by Q. This of course we date 1598; (iv) ll. 92–
164, where we return to the lovers and the first draft.
It will be observed that §§ ii–iv give us 122 lines of
verse, which allowing for a little expansion in § iii in
1598 would cover about two pages of Shakespearian
MS. In other words, it is possible that in 1598 ll. 74–
91 were added in the margin of the existing MS to
replace deleted material of approximately the same
quantity; and it is curious to reflect that considerations
of space may have helped to determine their verse-
form.

S.D. Q. 'Enter Tytania Queene of Fairies, with
her traine.' F. following Q. 1619 omits the name
'Tytania.'

Another part of the wood etc. We change the *mise-en-
scène* here for the convenience of the reader, who would
be puzzled if 2. 1. and 2. 2. were run together. In the
Elizabethan theatre no change was needed except the
drawing aside of the traverse before the inner-stage, at
the back of which was Titania's bower. Shakespeare
clearly regarded the front stage as some kind of clearing
(cf. 3. 2. 25 'at a stump here' and 3. 2. 417 'uneven
way'), and the inner-stage as the grassy plot beneath
the oak-tree (cf. 1. 2. 102; 3. 1. 3), which stood at
the back of the clearing. For instance, Titania's com-

mand 'lead him to my bower' at the end of 3. 1. indicates an exit from the front to the inner stage followed by a closing of the traverse.

2. *the third part of a minute* 'This quaint division of time exactly suits the character of the speaker and her diminutive world' (Halliwell).

8. S.D. Q. 'Fairies sing.'

21. Q. heads this verse '1 Fai.' F. '2 Fairy.'

25. *melody* Q. 'melody, &c.'—the full refrain not being repeated.

33. Q. heads this '2 Fai.' F. '1 Fairy.'

34. S.D. Q. 'Enter Oberon.' F. adds 'Shee fleepes' at the end of the last line of the song. Neither gives an 'exeunt' for the fairies.

42. S.D. Q. 'Enter Lyfander: and Hermia.' Q. gives no 'exit' for Oberon.

46. *comfort* (Q. 1619) Q. 'comfor'

47. *Be't* (Pope) Q. 'Bet it' The compositor has set up the contracted form and then expanded it! v. p. 79.

51. *good* (Q. 1619) Q. 'god' This is apparently an occasional Shakespearian spelling. It occurs in *Troil.* I. 3. 169, and elsewhere in expressions like 'god-morrow,' 'god-night.'

54. *Love takes the meaning* etc. 'Love enables lovers to understand each other's true meaning' (Chambers). v. G. 'conference.'

55. *is knit* (Q. 1619) Q. 'it knit'

65. *modesty:* We follow the Q. pointing here. All edd. since Theobald have read 'Lie further off; in human modesty,'

73. S.D. Q. 'Enter Pucke.' F. adds 'They fleepe.'

74–91. Q. assigns these lines to 'Puck.' Cf. head-note and pp. 87–91.

85. *Near this lack-love* etc. The scansion of this line has perplexed the prosodists, who have forgotten the dramatist in their concern for the poet. Assuredly the line, which though harsh and drawling can be spoken

rhythmically without any difficulty, admirably expresses
the contempt of the 'shrewd and knavish sprite' as he
points at Lysander.

91. S.D. Q. 'Exit.'/'Enter Demetrius and Helèna
running.'

95. S.D. F. 'Exit Demetrius.' Q. omits.

112. *Nature shows an art* Q. 'nature ſhewes arte'
F. 'nature her ſhewes art' Malone, followed by many
mod. edd., reads 'Nature shows her art', i.e. he treats
the F. reading as a misprint. Others follow F2, which
reads 'nature here shews art'. Neither F1 nor F2 can
of course claim any authority, and it seems to us more
likely that the omitted word was 'an', which coming
before 'art' would easily be overlooked by the compositor. The line clearly lacks a syllable; and 'nature
shows an art' would seem more Shakespearian than
'nature shows her art.' Cf. *Wint.* 4. 4. 90 'over that
art/Which you say adds to nature, is an art/That nature
makes.' v. G. 'art.'

117. *What though he love* etc. Surely Shakespeare
wrote this line very early in his career?

126. *ripe not to reason* 'ripe' is of course a verb here.

127. *the point of human skill* the pinnacle of human
knowledge. v. G. 'point,' 'skill.'

129–30. *your eyes…love's richest book* Cf. *L.L.L.*
4. 3. 298–300:

> From women's eyes this doctrine I derive—
> They are the ground, the books, the academes,
> From whence doth spring the true Promethean fire.

142, 152, 164. S.D. Q. 'Exit.'

3. 1.

We ascribe the whole of this scene, which opens with
the clowns and continues with *Robin* speech-headings,
to 1594 (v. p. 96), though we suspect that Shakespeare

added at least one fresh touch to it in 1598 (v. note l. 83).
It runs to 182 lines in the Q., which allowing for the
prose gives us about three pages of Shakespearian MS.

S.D. Q. 'Enter the Clownes.'

2. *marvellous*   Q. 'maruailes'—a Shakespearian
spelling; cf. 4. 1. 24, and 2 *Hen. IV*, 5. 1. 38. In *Ham.*
2. 1. 3 we get the variant 'meruiles.'

6. *Peter Quince!* Q. 'Peeter Quince?' The '?' as
so often in the old texts stands for '!'. Exclamation marks
were scarce with printers of this period; and the printer
of the present quarto only possessed a few in an italic
fount which he used occasionally.

22. *eight and six* v. G. Bottom protests; he cannot
have too much of a good thing.

27. *yourselves* (F.) Q. 'your felfe'

28. *a lion among ladies* Cf. pp. 94–5.

46. *Doth the moon shine* etc. Q. assigns this to 'Sn.',
which some edd., following F2, interpret 'Snug'; but
we get another 'Sn.' speech-heading at l. 109 immediately after 'Enter Snout', and there is no evidence
that Shakespeare remembered Snug's existence during
this scene.

49. F. gives the S.D. 'Enter Pucke.' here; v.
p. 157.

50–3. *it doth shine that night...at the casement* Some
have found a difficulty here, e.g. Chambers writes: 'The
wedding-day is...the day of a new moon (1. 1. 3–10).
Now, a new moon sets almost with the sun; and yet there
is moon enough for the rehearsal (1. 2. 94–5), and it will
even shine in at the casement of the great chamber
window for the performance (3. 1. 51–3).' To which it
may be replied (i) that as a matter of fact the moon did
not play a part, except by proxy, in the performance,
and (ii) that the whole play is bathed in moonlight
(cf. 1. 1. 210; 2. 1. 60, 141; 3. 1. 164, 189 etc.), and
yet the action takes place on exactly those nights in the
month when the moon is least visible. Shall we say that

Shakespeare cared nothing for astronomical exactitude—
he left that to Quince? Hardly, since the trouble all
arises from 1.1.1–11, which was probably added at the
time of a revision (cf. head-note 1.1. and 1.1. 2–3 note).

51. *Why, then* etc. Q. heads this speech 'Cet.' which
is probably nothing but a misprint for 'bot' (i.e. Bottom),
though it is a curious one not easy to explain.

64. *and let* (Collier) Q. 'or let'—an easy misprint
after the twice-repeated 'or' above.

71. S.D. Q. 'Enter Robin.' F. does not delete; cf.
note l. 49 above. Ll. 72 and 101 are headed 'Rob.'
v. head-note.

75. *actor too* Q. 'actor to'

76–98. The rehearsal does not tally with the play as
finally performed. 'The inconsistency is quite easily
understood. It would be very tedious for Shakespeare's
audience to go a second time over the same bit of burlesque' (Chambers). Cf. note 1. 2. 55–8.

77. *flowers ha' odious* Q. 'flowers of odious' It is
dangerous to correct Bottom-Pyramus; but we think the
'of' here is undoubtedly due to the compositors who in
this text disliked abbreviated forms (v. p. 79). Shakespeare, we believe, wrote 'a' which might mean either
'have' or 'of.' Collier (2nd ed.) reads 'have'. Cf. *L.L.L.*
5. 2. 17 (note).

78. *Odorous, odorous* (Collier) Q. 'Odours, odorous'
F. 'Odours, odours' Cf. *Ado*, 3. 5. 15 'Comparisons
are odorous.'

82. S.D. Q. 'Exit.' F. 'Exit. Pir.' v. p. 156.

83. *A stranger Pyramus* etc. Q. assigns this to 'Quin.'
and F. corrects. The Q. error is interesting. Possibly
'pu' has been taken for 'qu' by the compositor; and
if so, it follows that the line was added in the margin
at the time of the 1598 revision, seeing that Puck's other
speeches in this scene are assigned to 'Robin.'

84. *Must I speak now?* Q. heads this, and the rest of
Flute's speeches in this scene, 'Thyf.' Shakespeare has

forgotten that he assigned Thisby's part to Flute in 1. 2. and does not recollect it right up to the end of the play. Cf. head-note 4. 2. and 5. 1. 155 (note).

90. *Jew* We take this to be simply a playful diminutive of 'Juvenal,' v. G.

92. *Ninny's tomb* Cf. note 5. 1. 201.

93–6. '*Ninus' tomb,*' *man* etc. Q. prints this as verse; perhaps Shakespeare wrote it in short lines in his manuscript.

95. *cues and all* The 'cues' were, of course, included in the player's 'part.' v. G. 'part.'

97. S.D. Q. gives no entry. F. reads 'Enter Piramus with the Affe head' after l. 106. Cf. pp. 155–57.

98. *If I were fair, Thisby,* etc. We follow the Q. punctuation. What Bottom's part read, we presume, was 'If I were [i.e. true], fair Thisby, I were only thine.' But the blunder adds point to the transformation.

100. S.D. Q. gives no 'exeunt.' F. 'The Clownes all Exit.'

101–106. *I'll follow you* etc. 'Note the pelting, rattling staccato, which sounds like the explosion of a pack of Chinese firecrackers, at the heels of the flying clowns' (Furness).

106. S.D. Q. 'Exit.' F. adds 'Enter Piramus with the Affe head.' Cf. pp. 155–57.

108. S.D. Q. 'Enter Snowte.'

112. S.D. Q. 'Enter Quince.' Q. gives no 'exit' for Snout.

114. *translated* v. G. and 1. 1. 191. S.D. Q. 'Exit.'

118. *and will sing* (Q.) Q. 1619 'and I will fing' —which F. and most edd. follow.

119. *ousel* (Pope) Q. 'Woofell' The blackbird. For this song cf. Drayton, *Polyolbion*, xiii. 55–60.

122. *with little quill* i.e. with little pipe.

126–27. *Whose note* etc. Cf. the 'Cuckoo' song in *L.L.L.* Bottom's comment shows that he entirely misses the point.

136–39. *And yet, to say the truth...I can gleek upon occasion.* 'A gleek is rather a satirical than a waggish joke, and in this vein Bottom flatters himself he has just been rather successfully indulging' (Aldis . Wright). We suspect some topical reference here.

142. *mine owe turn* v. G. 'owe (adj.).'

145–46. *I am a spirit...tend upon my state* Fleay (*Life*, pp. 183–84) thinks that Shakespeare is here alluding to the following passage from Nashe's *Summer's Last Will* (acted 1592, pub. 1600): 'Eliza, England's beauteous queen,/On whom all seasons prosperously attend.' Shakespeare may be thinking of Elizabeth; but surely not necessarily of Nashe, seeing that 'Queen's weather' must have been as famous in Elizabethan as in Victorian days. It is curious how many little points suggest comparison between Titania and Elizabeth. Cf. pp. 100, 101, 103.

153. S.D. Q. 'Enter foure Fairyes.' F. 'Enter Peafe-bloſſome, Cobweb, Moth, Muſtard-ſeede, and foure Fairies.' v. pp. 154–55. For 'Moth,' v. G.

154. Q. prints *'Fairies.* Readie: and I, and I, and I. Where ſhall we goe?' This arrangement represents the swift appearance of the fairies, one after another, with beautiful precision.

166–69. Q. prints '1. *Fai.* Haile mortall, haile./ 2. *Fai.* Haile./3. *Fai.* Haile.' Capell first arranged as in our text. It will be noticed that in what follows Bottom has no word of welcome for Moth. It looks as if Shakespeare planned the scene in 1594 for four fairies but for some reason found three more convenient in 1598. The point has not escaped Fleay (v. *Life*, p. 183).

186. *you of more* (Collier) Q. 'you more' Most edd. read 'your more' with F3; but the compositor has apparently simply omitted the 'of' which Bottom has twice used already (ll. 173, 179).

188. *lead him to my bower* v. head-note 2. 2. S.D.

191. *enforcéd* i.e. violated.

192. *Tie up my love's tongue* (Pope) Q. 'Tye vp my louers tongue' The love-juice had latched Titania's eyes not her ears.

S.D. Q. 'Exit.'

3. 2.

This long scene, much of which belongs, as we believe, to the first draft, chiefly concerns the lovers, and may have seemed tedious to Shakespeare in 1598. At any rate it is clear that the text has been revised. We divide the scene into six sections: (i) ll. 1–40, which we think was written in 1594, judging by the style, the 'Robin goodfellow' in the Q. S.D., and the *Rob*. prefix at l. 38. On the other hand the *Puck* prefix at l. 6 suggests that Puck's long speech was partially revised in 1598, possibly in order to shorten it; (ii) ll. 41–101, lover-material, from the first draft, containing what we take to be two 'cuts,' at l. 49 and ll. 80–1; (iii) ll. 102–121, a brief passage, dealing with the 'western flower' and contain- ing two *Puck* prefixes and a S.D. 'Enter Puck', which we ascribe to 1598, supposing that it may have been written in the margin; (iv) ll. 122–194, lover-material belonging to the first draft; (v) ll. 195–400, which we conjecture may have been 4 pp. (of 51 ll.) partially recopied and revised in 1598, but containing at least one 'cut' at l. 257. Cf. note l. 195 and the *Puck* speech- headings in ll. 345–400. The end of the section is marked by the crowding of ll. 396–99, in order as we believe to get them into the foot of one MS page, and the sudden change to *Rob*. at l. 402; (vi) ll. 401–63, probably written in 1594, since all Puck's speeches are headed *Rob*. and his concluding speech makes no reference to the 'flower.' Moreover since this section runs to 59 lines in Q. (v. note ll. 448–63) it may repre- sent one more page of Shakespearian MS.

S.D. Q. 'Enter King of Fairies, and Robin good- fellow.' F. 'Enter King of Pharies, folus.' F. prints 'Enter Pucke.' after l. 3. v. p. 156.

5. *night-rule* v. G. 'rule.'

6. *My mistress* etc. Q. heads this speech 'Puck', but ll. 38 and 42 are headed 'Rob.' Cf. head-note.

13. *sort* v. G.

17. *noll* Q. 'nole'—a common 16th c. spelling.

19. *mimic* (F.) Q. 'Minnick' v. G.

24. *fly;* Q.'fly,' 25. *falls*— Q.'falles:'—transposed pointing.

25. *at a stump* (Johnson) Q. 'at our ſtampe' Johnson very aptly quotes from Drayton's *Nimphidia*, a poem deeply indebted to this play:

> A stump doth trip him in his pace.
> Down fell poor Hob upon his face,
> And lamentably tore his case
> Among the briars and the brambles.

He also writes 'Fairies are never represented stamping, or of a size that should give force to a stamp, nor could they [the mechanicals] have distinguished the stamps of Puck from those of their own companions.' The fact that Robin *is* represented as stamping in Scot's *Discovery of Witchcraft* (ed. Nicholson, p. 67), and that Oberon and Titania 'rock the ground' as they dance in this very play (4. 1. 85), annihilates part of Johnson's argument, and has thrown discredit upon his conjectural reading. Yet the Q. reading is surely nonsense. What is the point of making the clown fall head-over-heels as Puck stamps? Why does the stamp affect one clown only? For what reason does Puck suddenly use the editorial 'our'? On the other hand, 'at a stump here o'er and o'er one falls' gives just the incident in which Puck, with his three-foot stool pranks, would delight; and the misprint 'stampe' < 'stumpe' belongs to one of the commonest types of error in the canon (v. T.I. p. xli, and Sh. Hand, p. 118). As for the 'our', it cannot be right in any event, and has no serious defenders. We suggest that Shakespeare wrote the *a* like *œ* (v. Sh. Hand, p. 120 and Plate v), and that the compositor took it for 'o', the contracted form of 'our'. Cf. notes 4. 1. 216; 5. 1. 34.

38. *finished too* Q. 'finiſht to'

40. S.D. Q. 'Enter Demetrius and Hermia.'

46. *curse...* Q. 'curſe.'   47. *sleep,* Q. 'ſleepe;'—transposed pointing.

48–9. *Being o'er-shoes...kill me too* Q. prints this as one line. This fact, the broken l. 49 and its occurrence in the midst of a passage of rhyming couplets point unmistakably to abridgment. Cf. head-note. For 'o'er-shoes' cf. *Two Gent.* 1. 1. 24–6.

49. *me too* Q. 'mee to'   52. *From* Q. 'Frow'

53–5. *This whole earth ... Antipodes* Furnivall rightly regards this 'comical comparison of the moon tumbling through the earth' as a mark of youthful composition. v. G. 'whole,' 'Antipodes.'

80–1. Q. prints 'And from thy hated preſence part I: ſee me no more;/Whether he be dead or no.' The irregular lining and the awkward proximity of 'never to see me more' (l. 79) and 'See me no more' (l. 81) strongly suggest abridgment.

80. *part I so* (Pope) Q. 'part I:' Crowding in the MS (v. previous note) and the similarity of 'so' and 'see' would account for the omission.

81. S.D. Q. 'Exit.'

85. *sleep* (Rowe) Q. 'ſlippe'—an interesting spelling, not found in N.E.D. or Wyld, *Hist. Coll. Eng.* Cf. the 'ship-sheep' quibble, *Two Gent.* 1. 1. 72–3; *L.L.L.* 2. 1. 217.

86. *pay,* Q. 'pay;'

87. S.D. Q. 'Ly doune.' v. p. 80.

88–99. *What hast thou done?* etc. If our textual analysis be correct (v. head-note) this is the only Oberon-Robin passage in the text from the first draft.

92–3. *Then fate o'er-rules* etc. This sententious comment in 'Robin's' mouth is strangely out of keeping with Puck's character. Cf. note ll. 88–99 above.

97. *sighs of love...fresh blood dear* Cf. 'blood-consuming sighs' 2 *Hen. VI*, 3. 2. 61; 'lose...blood with love' *Ado*, 1. 1. 235; 'dry sorrow drinks our blood' *Rom*. 3. 5. 59. Every sigh was supposed at this time to cost a drop of blood.

101. *Swifter...Tartar's bow* Perháps derived from Golding's trans. of Ovid's *Metamorphoses*, bk. x. 'Swift as arrow from a Turkye bow.' The Oriental bow, of three-ply construction, was more powerful than the English bow (v. Sh. Eng. ii. 379).

S.D. Q. gives no 'exit.' Q. 1619 supplies one.

102–21. *Flower of this purple dye* etc. These 20 lines of short trochaic couplets might easily have been written in the margin at the time of the 1598 revision (v. head-note). Once again possibly, considerations of space may have helped to determine the verse-form. Cf. head-note 2. 2.

107. *the Venus of the sky* Cf. l. 61 above.

109. S.D. Q. 'Enter Puck.' Ll. 110, 118 are headed *Puck.* and *Pu.* in Q. v. head-note.

119. *alone* v. G.

121. S.D. Q. 'Enter Lyſander, and Helena.'

124–25. i.e. vows so born appear all truth in their nativity.

136. S.D. F. 'Awa.' Cf. p. 158.

144. *princess of pure white* v. G. 'princess.'

150. *mock me too* Q. 'mocke mee to'

164. *And here* Q. 'And heare'

171. *to her...sojourned* The 'to' has puzzled edd. but v. G. 'sojourn to.'

176. S.D. Q. 'Enter Hermia.'

195. *Injurious Hermia, most ungrateful maid* Note the sudden change from couplets to blank verse, and blank running verse into paragraphs, rarely end-stopped and making pauses in the middle of the line. It seems more than possible that we are dealing with revision work here. Chambers suspects that the whole of the

section (177–344) may be 'later work.'   Cf. head-note (v), and pp. 86, 92.

204. *needles* pronounced 'neelds' or 'neels,' and very possibly written so in the 'copy' (cf. p. 79, and N.E.D. 'needle').

first, like (Theobald) Q. 'firſt life' Cf. *f* and *k* Sh. Hand, Plate v.

215. *rend* (Rowe) Q., F. 'rent.'

220. *at your words* F. 'at your paſſionate words' which all edd. follow. v. p. 159. We suspect that a 'cut' may have occurred here.

225. *Who even but now* etc. We retain the Q. brackets in this indignant speech. They are all expressive and give us the rapid changes in Helena's intonation: l. 239, for instance, is, we think, intended to be uttered with a sob.

236. *by this*. Q. 'by this,' The comma suggests that part of Hermia's original speech may have been can-celled.

250. *prayers* (Theobald) Q. 'praiſe' The emenda-tion is accepted by all, though the misprint is not easy to explain.

252. *for thee*, Q. 'for thee;'

257. Q. reads 'No, no: heele' F. 'No, no, Sir,' and there have been many conjectures. Our own belief is that the words are a fragment of a cancelled passage and that they should be omitted. N.B. the line is a syllable short.

260. *Hang off* Q. 'Hang of'

279. *Therefore* Q. 'Thefore'

question, doubt (Pope) Q. 'queſtion, of doubt'

282. *canker-blossom* v. G.

299. *gentlemen* (Q. 1619) Q. 'gentleman'

313. *too* (F.) Q. 'to'

323. *When she is* Q. 'O, when ſhe is' F. 'O when ſhe's' which all edd. follow. There seems no point in this 'O', and we take it to be the *e* of the 'Hele.' speech-

heading which, misread as *o*, has crept into the text. Cf. the frequent instances of this kind of thing in *L.L.L.* (v. notes 2. 1. 211; 3. 1. 142; 4. 3. 279, 285).

329. *knot-grass* a very apt comparison, v. G.

338. S.D. Q. gives no 'exeunt.' Q. 1619 reads 'Exit.' F. reads 'Exit Lyſander and Demetrius.'

344. S.D. Q. 'Exeunt.' F. omits, because the compositor skips a line: it adds however 'Enter Oberon and Pucke.'

345–400. All Puck's speeches in this section have *Puck* speech-headings. Cf. 'this herb' (l. 366) and head-note (v).

348. *should* Q. 'ſhoud'   363. *thus,* Q. 'thus;'

389. *I with the morning's love...sport* i.e. I have dallied with Aurora. Cf. G. 'fairy time.'

392–93. Cf. *Son.* 33 'Gilding pale streams with heavenly alchemy.'

394. *notwithstanding* Q. 'notwiſtanding'

396–99 are printed as two lines in Q. and presumably Shakespeare wrote them so in order to crowd them into the foot of a page. v. head-note (v).

400. S.D. Q. 'Enter Lyſander.'

401–63. In this section we return to *Robin* speech-headings; the speeches belonging to the 'voices' being, of course, headed *Rob.* in Q.

403–404. Q. prints 'Follow...ground' as one line. S.D. Q. 'Enter Demetrius.'

406. *Speak! In some bush?* (Capell) Q. 'Speake in ſome buſh.'

412. S.D. Q. 'Exeũt.' F. 'Exit.'

416. Against this line F. prints the words 'ſhifting places' as a S.D. v. pp. 156–57.

418. S.D. F. 'lye down.'

420. S.D. Q. 'Robin, and Demetrius.' F. prefixes the word 'Enter'

426. *shalt* Q. 'ſhat'

430. S.D. Q. 'Enter Helena.'

436. S.D. Q. 'Sleepe.'

441. S.D. F. 'Enter Hermia.' Q. omits.

448–63. *On the ground...all shall be well* Q. prints this in 9 lines.

451. *To your eye* (Rowe) Q. 'your eye'

463. S.D. Q. gives no 'exit' for Puck.

F. prints 'They fleepe all the Act' at the end of this scene. This S.D. implies that the lovers are to 'sleep' in full view of the audience during the interval—an absurdity for which Shakespeare cannot be responsible. Cf. pp. 158–59 and T.I. § 3.

4. 1.

Probably most of the scene was composed in 1594 though certain parts look like first draft material recopied, e.g. the prose-lining of Titania's speeches ll. 27, 34–5 suggests copying, while it seems likely that Hippolyta was introduced into the scene for the first time in 1594, cf. notes ll. 185, 195, head-note 1. 1. and 1. 1. 123–26. On the other hand, though there are *Robin* prefixes throughout, we think the 1598 revision affected the scene at three points (v. notes ll. 70–4, 86–91, 164–66), one certainly and another possibly connected with the 'flower.' Cf. pp. 96–7.

S.D. Q. 'Enter Queene of Faieries, and Clowne, and Faieries: and the king behinde them.' All Bottom's speeches are prefixed *Clown* in this scene. For the triple 'and' cf. note 1. 1. 19.

8, 10, 12, etc. *Monsieur* (Rowe) Q. 'Mounfieur' —which is just the old form, and was not intended as a 'mistake' on Bottom's part.

20. *leave your curtsy* i.e. put on your hat. Mustard-seed is making a profound bow; and Bottom, like other Elizabethan grandees, shows his affability by excusing such obeisances in his inferiors. Cf. *L.L.L.* 5. 1. 95; *Ham.* 5. 2. 108. Most edd. read 'courtesy', but the Q. gives us 'curtfie'

22–3. *help Cavalery Cobweb* etc. Bottom—or is it Shakespeare?—has forgotten that Peaseblossom and not Cobweb is to do the scratching.

24. *marvellous* Q. 'maruailes' Cf. note 3. 1. 2.

27. *What, wilt...love?*   34–5. *I have...new nuts* Q. prints both these speeches as prose. The first might be accidental; the second we must attribute to prose-arrangement in the 'copy.' It is possible that the dialogue was originally all in verse and that Shakespeare, in translating Bottom's 'part' into prose, did not trouble to preserve the verse-arrangement in Titania's shorter speeches.

29. S.D. F. 'Muſicke Tongs, Rurall Muſicke.' v. pp. 157–58.

30. *desir'st* (Rowe) Q. 'deſireſt'

35. *fetch thee thence new nuts* (Hanmer) Q. 'fetch thee newe nuts' Many suggestions have been offered for the missing word; the similarity of 'thee' and 'thence' renders the latter a likely word to have been omitted by the compositor.

40. *all ways* (Theobald)   Q. 'alwaies'

S.D. Q. gives no 'exeunt.'

41. *woodbine* We suggest *bindweed*. Since 'wood-bine' *is* honeysuckle, and is so identified by Shakespeare in *Much Ado* (3. 1. 8, 30), to say nothing of the 'luscious woodbine' in 2. 1. 251 above, the Q. reading has puzzled every editor; but most agree with Gifford that Shakespeare meant 'bindweed,' i.e. the convolvulus, a parallel from Jonson's *Vision of Delight*:

> behold!
> How the blue bindweed doth itself infold
> With honey-suckle, and both these intwine
> Themselves with bryony and jessamine,

being almost conclusive. How came the error? We believe that Shakespeare not only meant but actually wrote 'bind weed,' that he formed, however, his *d* like *e* and his *e*'s like *o*'s, as he frequently did (v. T.I. pp. xli-

xlii and Sh. Hand, p. 119, Plate v), and that the compositor therefore thought he saw 'bine wood' in the MS and took it as an error for 'wood-bine.' Capell and others take 'woodbine' in apposition to 'honeysuckle,' and 'entwist' as absolute. Apart from the ruined parallelism and the general harshness of construction involved, this interpretation is, we think, definitely put out of court by two considerations: (i) The word 'entwist' (= interweave) suggests two creepers twining together; Shakespeare uses 'enring' for the creeper clinging to a standard. (ii) It is obviously the unsavoury Bottom who is the 'sweet honeysuckle'; the apposition-theory would make Titania address the description to herself!

44. S.D. Q. 'Enter Robin goodfellow.' F. adds 'and Oberon.'—ignoring the entry for 'the king behinde them' at the head of the scene.

49. *with her:* Q. 'with her.'

51. *flowers:* Q. 'flowers.'

53. *pearls,* Q. 'pearles;'

54. *flowerets* Q. 'flouriets'

64. *off* Q. 'of'

65. *other* Cf. *L.L.L.* I. I. 158 'Suggestions are to other as to me.'

70–4. *Be as...queen.* These five lines were, we think, added to the MS in 1598. They refer to 'Dian's bud' and 'Cupid's flower' and there would be room for five lines at right angles in the margin. Note (i) that they are not dramatically essential and (ii) that ll. 69 and 74 both end with 'queen' to rhyme with 'seen' (l. 75).

72. *o'er* (Theobald) Q. 'or'

81. Q. 'Then common fleepe: of all thefe, fine the fenfe.' Note how the misprint 'fine' for 'fiue' has affected the Q. punctuation. Theobald first read 'five'

82. *ho!* Q. 'howe' Cf. Sh. Hand, p. 140. S.D. F. 'Mufick ftill.' (v. p. 158). The prompter seems to have been puzzled by the two calls for music in ll. 82, 84.

86–91. *Now thou...all in jollity* These words fore-
tell the dance and song at the end of 5. 1., and must
belong to the same revision as they. We conjecture that
they were added in 1598. Once again there is room in
the margin for six lines at right angles to the column
of verse.

95. *the night's* (Q. 1619) Q. 'nights' Some edd.
read 'nightës'

100. After this line F. gives the S.D. 'Sleepers Lye
ftill.' v. p. 158.

101. S.D. Q. 'Exeunt.'/'Enter Thefeus and all his
traine. Winde horne,' F. 'Exeunt.'/'Winde Hornes.'/
'Enter Thefeus, Egeus, Hippolita and all his traine.'

102–26. *Go one of you* etc. This lovely passage was,
we think, added to the text in 1594. Cf. note l. 185
below.

103. *our observation* Cf. ll. 131–32 below, and
1. 1. 167.

107. S.D. Q. gives none.

116. *Seemed* (F2) Q. 'Seeme'—*e*:*d* misprint.

118. *My hounds...Spartan kind* The hounds of
Sparta were celebrated; cf. Vergil, *Georgics*, iii. 405.
Possibly Shakespeare learnt the fact from Golding's
'Ovid,' e.g. 'This latter was a hounde of Crete, the other
was of Spart.' He took the idea of Theseus as a hunts-
man from Chaucer's *Knightes Tale*; cf. ll. 1673–95.
But the dogs were of English breed, and Theseus an
Elizabethan gentleman.

122–23. *matched in mouth like bells,/Each under each*
i.e. with different notes, like a chime of bells. Edd.
quote Markham's *Country Contentments*: 'If you would
have your kennell for sweetnesse of cry, then you must
compound it of some large dogges, that have deepe
solemne mouthes, and are swift in spending, which
must, as it were, beare the base in the consort, then a
double number of roaring, and loud ringing mouthes,
which must beare the counter-tenour; then some hollow,

plaine, sweet mouthes, which must beare the meane or middle part; and soe with these three parts of musicke you shall make your cry perfect.' But J. W. Fortescue thinks this exaggerated (v. Sh. Eng. ii. 347).

127. *this is my* (Q. 1619) Q. 'this my'

132. *rite* (Pope) Q. 'right'—a common spelling.

137. S.D. Q. 'Shoute within: they all ſtart vp. Winde hornes.' F. 'Hornes and they wake./Shoute within, they all ſtart vp.' It seems probable that 'Shoute within' was the original form of the réveillé, rejected later for the more appropriate 'hornes.' It may be noticed that Egeus' 'It is, my lord' stands now as a broken line, which 'Go, bid the huntsmen *shout*' would complete.

138. *past;* Q. 'paſt.'

140. S.D. Capell 'He and the rest kneel to Theseus.' Furness describes this as a 'very superfluous stage-direction.' On the contrary, without it a reader might imagine that Theseus' injunction, 'I pray you all, stand up,' had something to do with the awakening of the lovers.

145–46. *reply amazedly, Half sleep, half waking* 'I am inclined to think that both "sleep" and "waking" are here substantives, and are loosely connected with the verb "reply"; just as we find in *M.W.W.* 3. 2. 62 "He speaks holiday"; *Tw. Nt.* 1. 5. 115 "He speaks nothing but madman"' (Aldis Wright).

152. *law*— Q. 'lawe,' Q. 1619 'corrects' this by printing a period for the comma, and reading 'might be' for 'might' in l. 151.

164–66. Q. arranges '(But by ſome power it is) my loue,/To Hermia (melted as the ſnowe)/Seemes...idle gaude,' It is remarkable that the only piece of overrun verse in this speech should be wrongly divided in the Q. We suggest that it was written in the margin during the 1598 revision to take the place of a longer cancelled passage. Possibly the original version referred to the

'power' in such terms as were ill-suited to the 'little
western flower'; cf. pp. 89–90.

165. *Melted as the snow* etc. Chambers writes 'I
doubt if this line can be scanned without emendation';
and Furness 'The irregularity of the lines possibly indicates an obscurity in the MS.' Staunton conj. 'All
melted' for 'melted,' and this is palaeographically
possible, if we suppose 'Herm.al melted' taken for
'Hermia (melted' v. previous note.

171. *saw* (Steevens) Q. 'fee' Curiously enough we
get the same error, twice, in *L.L.L.* 4. 1. 68, 69 (v.
notes). Can Shakespeare himself have been responsible?

172. *in sickness* (Farmer) Q. 'a ficknesse' Cf. *Oth.*
1. 3. 400 'a double' < 'in double'

177. *hear* (Q. 1619) Q. 'here'

185. *Come, Hippolyta* Q. prints this with l. 184. It
is to be noted that there is no mention of Hippolyta in
the Q. S.D. at l. 101; and she certainly appears to be an
afterthought here. Possibly she did not appear at all in
this scene in the first draft; and if so ll. 102–126 were
added in 1594, as from their style they may well have
been.

S.D. Q. gives no 'exeunt.' Q. 1619 'Exit.' F. 'Exit
Duke and Lords.'

190. *found* Q. 'fonnd'

190–91. *like a jewel, Mine own,* etc. Helena feels
like one who finds a jewel in the road. Is Demetrius
really hers, she asks, or will not some 'rightful owner'
turn up to claim him?

191–92. *Mine own...seems to me* Two broken lines,
which no amount of tinkering can make to scan. F.
cuts the knot by omitting the words 'Are you...are
awake?' which are superfluous to the sense and destroy
the rhythm. The trouble probably arose from careless
abridgment of the text at this point.

195. If Hippolyta be an afterthought (v. note l. 185)
this line must have been added later, in revision. Note

that Lysander ignores the ladies' words and continues Demetrius' theme: 'And *he* did bid us...'

197–98. *Why then...our dreams* Q. prints as prose, which suggests revision or careless copying once again.

198. *let us* (Q. 1619) Q. 'lets'
S.D. Q. gives no 'exeunt.' Q. 1619 'Exit.' F. 'Bottome wakes. Exit Louers.'

199. *When my cue comes* etc. Q. heads this 'Clo.' v. head-note S.D.

202. *bellows-mender* Q. 'bellowes menders'

205. *to say what* Q. 'to ſay; what' It was a trick of the compositors of this Q. to preface reported speech, or what they took to be reported speech, with a semi-colon.

209–10. *a patched fool* (F.) Q. 'patcht a foole'

211–13. *The eye of man* etc. Cf. 1 Cor. ii. 9 'Eye hath not seen, nor ear heard,' etc. It must be remembered that Bottom was a weaver, and therefore possibly of a Puritanical turn of mind. Cf. 1 *Hen. IV*, 2. 4. 146.

216. *our play* (Walker) Q. 'a Play' The reference to 'her death' (l. 218) proves that Bottom is thinking of *the* play and not 'a play.' For the converse misprint v. note 3. 2. 25; cf. also 5. 1. 34 (note).

218. *at her death* It is amazing that the acute Theobald missed the point of this and actually read 'after death', a reading which many edd. have thought plausible and Furness pronounced 'emendatio certissima.' Bottom's mind is full of the play—'When my cue comes, call me.' are his waking words—and of the part (if possible, parts) he is to perform therein. The 'Ballad of Bottom's Dream' fires his imagination and he sees himself rising at Thisby's death (which ends the play) and singing it (with that voice of his!) before the whole Court, the prostrate form of his love still lying at his feet.

S.D. Q. gives no 'exit.' F. supplies it.

4. 2.

We assign this, like the other clown-scenes, to 1594.
v. pp. 95–6.

S.D. Q. 'Enter Quince, Flute, Thisby and the
rabble.' F. reads 'Snout and Starueling' for 'and the
rabble.' Shakespeare has forgotten that Flute and Thisby
are the same person, and distributes the speeches before
Bottom's entry between 'Quin.', 'Flut.', and 'Thyf.'
(Cf. note 3. 1. 84 and *Ado*, pp. 95–7.) F. alters the
'Flut.' speech-heading to 'Staru.' and all edd. have
followed suit.

4. *transported* i.e. 'translated,' for which v. **G.**

11. *too* (Q. 1619) Q. 'to'

14. S.D. Q. 'Enter Snug, the Ioyner.'

22. S.D. Q. 'Enter Bottom.'

24. *courageous* Quince means 'brave' in the sense
of 'splendid.' Cf. Miranda's 'O brave new world!'
Temp. 5. 1. 184.

25. S.D. Capell supplies this.

27. *not true Athenian* So Q. F. 'no true Athenian'
which all edd. follow. There is no difference in sense.
Cf. *Acts* xvii. 21. 'Bottom's anxiety at once to tell his
tale and to keep up the mystery of it, is very humorous'
(Chambers).

34. *our play is preferred* i.e. recommended, put forward (v. N.E.D. 'prefer' 4). Philostrate, the master of
the revels, had placed it on his select list.

40. S.D. Q. gives no 'exeunt.'

5. 1.

We have already found proof of revision in the
irregular verse-lining at the beginning of this scene
(v. pp. 80–6) and in the *Puck-Robin* variation at the
end (v. pp. 87–8); we have now to show that the
same revision has affected the scene throughout. And
here our principal clue is a second variation in speech-
headings, namely the sudden change from *The.* and

Hip. to *Duk.* and *Dutch.* about halfway through the
dialogue. Fleay long ago pointed out this anomaly and
attributed it to revision (cf. *Life*, pp. 182–83). But,
without giving any reasons, he declared the *Duk.* and
Dutch. headings 'anterior in date' to *The.* and *Hip.*,
though, as we have found in previous texts, Shakespeare's
invariable tendency was exactly the reverse; that is to
say, apparently through sheer inattention he substituted generic titles for proper names when he was
revising (cf. *Ado*, pp. 95–7 and *L.L.L.* pp. 111–13).
We take the *Duke* and *Duchess* prefixes, therefore, as
indications that the text has been worked over wherever
they occur. In a word, the scene has evidently been
recast at the beginning, in the middle and at the end;
and since the end was undoubtedly revised in 1598, it
is natural to suppose that the rest of the scene was revised at the same time. A consideration of the Q. text
of 5.1., section by section, will, we think, make it clear
that this is actually what happened.

(i) ll. 1–84. These lines, we have seen reason for
thinking, constituted a page of first draft material, with
marginal additions belonging to 1598. Had the irregularly lined portions been added in 1594 they would have
been copied out with the rest and the lining rectified,
if our assumption of a fair copy in 1594 be correct
(v. p. 96). In any event the style and substance of
the additions make it practically certain that they were
written later than 1594.

(ii) ll. 85–182. In this section we begin the interlude
of the clowns, among them the redoubtable Lion. We
can, therefore, feel pretty confident that the material
does not go back beyond 1594 (v. pp. 95–6). Such
being the case, it is important to observe that all Theseus'
speeches at this point of the text are headed *The.*, with
one exception, while Hippolyta's are headed *Hip.* or
Hyp. The exception, l. 107 with a *Duke* prefix, is
significantly enough a broken line of verse, and as it

happens l. 92 is another broken line, while between these two broken lines is to be found a self-contained passage in mature Shakespearian verse with both feminine endings and mid-line pauses. In a word, we believe ll. 93–107 to be additional matter. Now an addition to a passage composed in 1594 is itself likely to have been composed later than 1594. It seems clear, in short, that this patch belongs to the 1598 revision, which suggests in turn that every speech with a *Duk.* or *Dutch.* prefix belongs to the same period. That the verse-lining in the addition is correct may easily be explained on the supposition that Shakespeare wrote it out on a slip in 1598 and glued it on to the original MS, to cover cancelled material.

(iii) ll. 183–368. Here we have neither irregular verse-division nor broken lines. Everything is in fact normal save that *Duke* and *Duchess* speech-headings run throughout the section. The interlude, begun in the previous section, proceeds on its way to the inevitable close, Snug among the rest distinguishing himself as Lion. Clearly the bulk of the dialogue belongs to the 1594 revision which gave us the clown-scenes which lead up to it. Nevertheless, the *Duke* and *Duchess* prefixes, if they mean anything at all, point to recasting and recopying in 1598. Nor are they the only clues which suggest this date. Theseus' comment in ll. 210–11 upon the acting profession—'The best in this kind are but shadows: and the worst are no worse, if imagination amend them'—was surely written in the same mood of confident self-banter as produced the jest at the expense of 'the poet' at the beginning of the scene. Even more significant is Theseus' condemnation of apologetic epilogues in ll. 354–56, which as we have already pointed out is most unlikely to have been written at the same time as the *Robin* epilogue, which we date 1594. Lastly, the Bergomask, which Theseus prefers to an epilogue, is obviously an antimasque intended, in the fashion of the time, as an introduction to the masque of fairies which follows immediately after, and belongs to 1598 as certainly as any part of the text. And if it be asked why Shakespeare in 1598 should recast the Pyramus and Thisby play, together with the accompanying dialogue, the answer is, we think, that the addition of the masque of fairies, including song and dance, would have prolonged the performance over-much, had not some corresponding abridgment been effected elsewhere. Our contention is, in brief, that Shakespeare cut down the mechanicals in order to make room for the fairies; and to abridge the clowns' play meant of course to recast it.

(iv) ll. 369–421. This we regard as entirely new material written expressly for the 1598 private performance, v. pp. 87–8.

(v) ll. 422–37. The *Robin* epilogue, which we attribute to 1594, and suppose that Shakespeare neglected to cancel in 1598 because it was written on a separate leaf.

S.D. Q. 'Enter Thefeus, Hyppolita, and Philoſtrate.' F. 'Enter Thefeus, Hippolita, Egeus and his Lords.' v. p. 159. *A curtain...lobby* For 'lobby' (= inner-stage) cf. *Ham.* 2. 2. 161. The inner-stage is required for 'Pyramus and Thisby' in the Q. text, though not in the F. version, which all edd. have hitherto followed; cf. notes ll. 347–49, 350 below. For *A fire* etc. v. note ll. 389–90.

1–84. v. pp. 80–6 for the Q. arrangement of these lines.

11. *a brow of Egypt* i.e. a gipsy's face.

13. *heaven;* Q. 'heauen.'

15. *unknown,* Q. 'Vnknowne:'

20. *that joy;* Q. 'that ioy.'

21–2. *Or in the night* etc. v. p. 83. R. G. White writes 'Would Shakespeare, after thus reaching the climax of his thought, fall a-twaddling about bushes and bears? Note too the loss of dignity in the rhythm.

I cannot even bring myself to doubt that these lines are interpolated' (v. Furness' *Variorum*); and Chambers, 'These lines are rather bald after what they follow. If the scene has been rewritten (cf. p. 86), perhaps we have here a survival from the earlier version.'

28. S.D. Q. 'Enter Louers; Lyſander, Demetrius, Hermia and Helena.' We suspect that Shakespeare wrote 'Enter Louers' and that the compositor or the prompter added the rest.

33. *three hours* It is noteworthy that the first draft speaks of '*a* torturing hour.' Cf. pp. 83–5.

34. *our after-supper* (F.) Q. 'Or after ſupper' The contracted 'oʳ' for 'our' has been read as 'or' in the cramped addition. Cf. note 3. 2. 25.

38. *Call Philostrate* Q. prints this with l. 37. F. 'Call Egeus' v. p. 159. Philostrate is Theseus' 'Master of the Revels' whose function it was, in Elizabethan days, to select the plays to be acted at Court from among those offered by the various companies for performance, by attending rehearsals and reading through the dramatic manuscripts (v. Feuillerat, *Le Bureau des Menus-Plaisirs*, p. 55).

39. *abridgment* v. G.

44–60. F. divides this speech between Lysander and Theseus, giving the former the 'brief' and the latter the comments upon it. Cf. p. 159.

44. *The battle with the Centaurs* The story of the battle, at which both Theseus and Hercules were present, between the Centaurs and the Lapithae is told in Ovid's *Metamorphoses*, bk. xii.

45, 49, 53, 57. Q. ends each of these lines with a question-mark.

48. *The riot of the tipsy Bacchanals* etc. An account of the death of Orpheus is given in Ovid's *Metamorphoses*, bk. xi. There is perhaps some topical allusion here.

52–5. *The thrice three Muses* etc. v. pp. 93–4.

59. *wondrous* Q. 'wodrous' for 'wŏdrous'

wondrous strange snow A much annotated passage; many conjectures being put forward in place of 'strange'. Some hold, however, that since 'strange' in Shakespeare often means 'prodigious' the text is in no need of alteration. For ourselves, we are convinced that after 'hot ice' Shakespeare would have given us some more startling epithet for 'snow' than the insipid 'strange'; and the word we think he probably wrote was *flaming* (first suggested by Joicey in *Notes and Queries*, Feb. 11, 1893), which in the cramped marginal addition we are dealing with might very easily be read as 'ſtraing', that being Shakespeare's spelling of the word 'strange' (v. Sh. Hand, pp. 127–28 and *L.L.L.* 5. 2. 759 note). The idea of 'flaming snow' may have come to Shakespeare from some traveller's tale of 'red snow' (v. N.E.D.) or from one of the pyrotechnic displays of which the age was so fond.

64. *tedious:* Q. 'tedious.'

66. *it is;* Q. 'it is.'   77. *for you:* Q. 'for you.'
81. *play:* Q. 'play.'   84. S.D. Q. gives no 'exit.'

89–105. *The kinder we* etc. Cf. *L.L.L.* 5. 2. 514–17, where the Princess develops the same argument in the same circumstances.

90. *mistake:* Q. 'miſtake.'

91–2. *noble respect Takes it in might, not merit* i.e. the consideration of noble minds takes the will for the deed. v. G. 'might.'

92. short line.

93–105. *Where I have come*, etc. v. head-note (ii). The lines have been almost universally regarded as a compliment to Elizabeth, and an allusion to the addresses made to her on her progresses by city dignitaries and, when she visited Oxford or Cambridge, by 'great clerks.' The allusion, we think, is certainly to some state visit to one of the universities, though not necessarily a royal visit. The Earl of Essex, for example, was formally installed as Chancellor of the University of Cambridge in the autumn of 1598 (Devereux, *Earls of Essex*, i. 503), too late, however, we think for this reference.

107. *Let him approach* broken line. Q. assigns this to 'Duk.', although all Theseus' speeches hitherto have been headed 'The.' and though the text returns to 'The.' at l. 118. Cf. head-note (ii).

S.D. Q. 'Enter the Prologue.' F. 'Flor. Trum.'/ 'Enter the Prologue. Quince.' The explanations which precede the play of 'Pyramus and Thisby,' if we include the speeches of Wall, Lion and Moonshine, are as long as the play itself. Shakespeare is laughing at the prologues and epilogues, the dumb-shows and presenters, which were fashionable at this time, and were convenient vehicles for information which the playwright had not skill enough to expound through the dialogue. Cf. Creizenach, *English Drama in the Age of Shakespeare*, pp. 276, 389.

108–17. *If we offend* etc. The punctuation in this speech is reproduced exactly as it stands in the Q., including the final comma which delightfully suggests the rising tone on which the stage-frighted Quince concludes. It is the only speech in the canon the punctuation of which edd. have hitherto treated with respect.

116–17. *by their show...like to know* These words announce the dumb-show to follow, and give us Shakespeare's opinion of dumb-shows and presenters in general. Cf. Hamlet's comment upon the 'fellow' who follows the dumb-show in his play: 'the players cannot keep counsel: they'll tell all' (*Ham.* 3. 2. 151–52).

117. S.D. Q. gives no 'exit' and theatrically none is needed since Quince is 'on' again at l. 125.

118. *points* v. G.

119–20. *rid...stop* v. G.

120. *lord—it* Q. 'Lord. It'

122. *his prologue* (F.) Q. 'this Prologue'

125. S.D. Q. 'Enter Pyramus, and Thisby, and Wall, and Moonefhine, and Lyon.' F. 'Tawyer with a Trumpet before them.'/'Enter Pyramus and Thisby, Wall, Moone-fhine, and Lyon.' v. p. 155.

126–50. *Gentles, perchance* etc. Q. heads this 'Prologue,' and it was certainly Quince's speech; but here he is playing the part of 'Presenter' to explain the 'dumb-show' which has just entered. He explains everything, at great length, and when he has finished, the play itself is seen to be superfluous. Cf. notes l. 107 S.D. and ll. 116–17. The punctuation of this speech is only less delicious than that of the 'prologue.'

153. S.D. Q. 'Exit Lyon, Thysby, and Moonefhine.' F. also reads this, but virtually cancels it by reading 'Exit all but Wall' after l. 150, a direction which all mod. edd. have followed. We adhere to the Q. arrangement.

155. *Snout* (F.) Q. 'Flute' Shakespeare has forgotten that he cast Flute for Thisby; the F. prompter corrects him. Cf. note 3. 1. 84.

162–63. *sinister...whisper*—an exquisite rhyme!

166. *partition* v. G.

167. F. reads 'Enter Pyramus' here; v. note l. 153 above.

183–86. Q. prints this as verse. Cf. note 3. 1. 93–6.

186. S.D. Q. 'Enter Thifby.'

190. *knit up in thee* (F.) Q. 'knit now againe' The F. reading makes good sense, though it is probably nothing more than a mere guess. The words 'now againe' could not possibly be a misprint for 'vp in thee', and we think it likely that the nonsense of the Q. conceals a true reading different from what the F. gives us.

193. *Thisby!* Q. prints this with l. 192.

195–98. *Limander ... Helen ... Shafalus ... Procrus* The last two are blunders for Cephalus and Procris, and the others are perhaps intended for Leander and Hero. Marlowe's *Hero and Leander* first appeared in 1593, and in the same year Th. Edwards' *Procris and Cephalus* was entered on the Stationers' Register.

201. *Ninny's tomb* A ludicrous error, 'ninny,' of course, meaning 'fool.' The tomb contains two ninnies before the end of the scene.

202. S.D. Q. gives no 'exeunt.'

204. S.D. Q. gives no 'exit.' F. reads 'Exit Clow.'

205. From this point onwards to the end of the scene all Theseus' and Hippolyta's speeches are headed 'Duk.' and 'Dutch.' in Q. v. head-note (iii).

Now is the moon used (Q.) Cf. ll. 136–37 above 'By moonshine did these lovers think no scorn/To meet at Ninus' tomb, there, there to woo.' Has Theseus some other meaning also? Demetrius' words seem to be a reply to a jest of some kind. F. reads 'Now is the morall downe', Pope altered 'morall' to 'mural', and the F. text, thus emended, has been followed by practically every mod. ed., though Aldis Wright declared that Pope's emendation had 'no evidence in its favour' and N.E.D. described it as 'a doubtful conjecture.'

207–208. *No remedy...warning* i.e. there's no help for it, when walls will take to themselves ears so unexpectedly.

210–11. *The best in this kind* etc. With this reference to players, cf. the fling at poets ll. 7–8, 12–17. Both are placed in the mouth of Theseus the practical man. Both are probably 1598 additions to the text. Cf. p. 85 and head-note (iii) above.

216. *beasts in, a* (Rowe) Q. 'beafts, in a'

a moon and a lion (Theobald) Q. 'a man and a Lyon' Mod. edd. have hesitated to adopt Theobald's emendation, but it effects so great an improvement in the text that it seems to us certain; and if Shakespeare happened to spell 'moon' with one *o* at this point the misprint would be explained; cf. *L.L.L.* 4. 3. 177 note. Theseus has just remarked that Quince's company of actors 'may pass for excellent men,' and the jest in the sudden transition from this to 'here come two noble *beasts* in' would be blunted altogether if we read 'a man and a lion.' One critic has objected that Theseus would not recognise the man with a lantern as 'moon,' the answer to which is that he does so in fact at l. 236, before Moonshine says a word.

S.D. Q. 'Enter Lyon, and Moone-fhine.'

217–24. *You ladies, you* etc. Cf. p. 95.

221. *as Snug* (Q.) F. 'one Snug' which all edd. follow, and have found themselves in serious difficulties in consequence. v. next note.

222. *A lion fell* Almost all mod. edd. interpret 'fell' as skin (after Barron Field) and read 'lion-fell', imagining some far-fetched jest about the skin being pregnant with the lion like a lion's dam. But if 'as' (Q.) be read for 'one' (F.) in l. 221 all is clear: he is a fell lion only in so far as he is Snug the Joiner and no farther.

227. *best...beast* a quibble, the two words in Shakespeare's day being much closer in sound than they are now.

237. *lanthorn...the hornèd moon* 'The form *lanthorn*,' the N.E.D. tells us, 'is probably due to popular etymology, lanterns having formerly been almost always made of horn.' Quince, or whoever wrote the play, evidently shared this belief.

239. *on his head* A reference to cuckoldry, jests upon which never failed to entertain the Elizabethans.

248. *in snuff* v. G. 'snuff.'

260. S.D. Q. 'Enter Thifby.' For our '*placard*' etc. cf. *Errors*, p. 81. Such placards were used in primitive stage-arrangements at this period.

262. S.D. F. 'The Lion roares, Thisby runns off.'

268. S.D. Q. 'Enter Pyramus.'

272. *gleams* (Knight) Q. 'beames'—the compositor probably catching the word from l. 270 just above.

274–85. Q. prints in eight lines.

286–87. Staunton quotes as parallel an old proverb 'He that loseth his wife *and* sixpence, hath lost a tester.'

303, 304. Q. gives no S.D.s.

305. *but one* Demetrius means, we suppose, 'unique.'

310. *and prove* (Q. 1619) Q. 'and yet prove'

311–12. *before Thisby* Q. 'before? Thifby'

314. S.D. Q. gives no entry. F. reads 'Enter Thisby' after l. 313.

317. *A mote* Q. 'A moth' Cf. G. 'moth' and *L.L.L.* 4. 3. 158 note.

balance, Q. 'ballance;'   318. *man*, Q. 'man;'

319. *warr'nt* Q. 'warnd' This is undoubtedly, we think, a Shakespearian form; it recurs, as 'warn't', in *Ham.* 1. 2. 243. *woman*, Q. 'woman;'

322. *means* Theobald and most later edd. read 'moans', quite unnecessarily. v. G. 'mean' and cf. *Two Gent.* 1. 2. 80–97 note.

323–46. Q. prints this in sixteen lines.

335. *O Sisters Three* etc. Malone noted that in these lines, and in Bottom's 'Approach, ye Furies fell', etc. (ll. 282 et seq.) 'the poet probably intended, as Dr Farmer observed to me, to ridicule a passage in *Damon and Pithias* by Richard Edwards, 1582: "Ye furies, all at once/On me your torments try:/Gripe me, you greedy griefs,/And present pangs of death;/You sisters three, with cruel hands/With speed come stop my breath."' See p. 94.

342. *Come, trusty sword* The traditional stage-business here is preserved for us in Edward Sharpham's play *The Fleir* (1607), wherein one character says of another 'Faith, like Thisbe in the play, a' has almost kil'd himselfe with the scabberd.'

346. Q. gives no entry here; but v. next note.

347–49. *Moonshine and Lion...and Wall too.* Why do Theseus and Demetrius mention these characters here? Lion's exit was at l. 268; Moonshine's at l. 303, and Wall's away back at l. 204; how then can they be '*left* to bury the dead'? The answer is that they re-enter at this point. They are needed for two purposes:

(i) to 'bury the dead' by drawing the traverse in front of Ninny's tomb (the inner-stage), so as to allow Pyramus and Thisby to make their exit unseen; and (ii) to offer the Epilogue and dance the Bergomask. The F. has obscured this; v. next note.

350. *No, I assure you* etc. F. heads this 'Bot.' and all edd. have followed suit. The only ed. indeed who seems even to have commented upon the difference between Q. and F. here is Collier: he writes: 'The Qq. give this speech to Lion. Perhaps such was the original distribution, but changed before F1 was printed, to excite laughter on the resuscitation of Pyramus.' We suggest that the change was made for theatrical rather than for dramatic reasons. If neither traverse nor inner-stage were available, what was to be done with the slain lovers, who must somehow be cleared away to make room for the Bergomask? The most effective solution was obviously for Pyramus to start up (resuscitating at the same time Thisby, whose tender form lay across his chest) and speak Lion's lines. The Q. arrangement, which represents Shakespeare's intentions, demands an inner-stage; the F. does not. Cf. pp. 158–59.

352–53. *Epilogue...Bergomask* We imagine that Lion was armed with a written 'epilogue,' for use if required, and that Wall and Moonshine dance the Bergomask (v. G.). Theseus is prologue-crammed and has no stomach for an epilogue (cf. note l. 107 S.D. and ll. 126–50 above). The Bergomask is the antimasque, introductory to the dance and song of the fairies with which the play closes.

360. Q. gives no S.D. here; but the pause for the dance is marked by the change from prose to verse in Theseus' speech. The verse, with its reference to midnight and the hint of 'fairy time' (v. G.), prepares us for the return of the fairies, and must have been written on the same occasion as what follows.

361. *told* The quibble on 'tolled' is obvious.

368. S.D. Q. 'Exeunt'/'Enter Pucke.'

370. *behowls* (Warburton) Q. 'beholds'—an *e*:*d* misprint. As Malone observed: 'The word "beholds" was, in the time of Shakespeare, frequently written "behoulds"...which probably occasioned the mistake.' Cf. the spellings 'withhoulds' (2. 1. 26) and 'hould' (2. 1. 55). Warburton's emendation has been accepted by all.

377. *Now it is the time of night* etc. Cf. 3. 2. 381–87 and *Ham.* 3. 2. 406–8:

'Tis now the very witching time of night
When churchyards yawn and hell itself breathes out
Contagion to this world.

382. *the triple Hecate's team* Ovid speaks of Diana as 'diva triformis' in *Metamorphoses*, vii. 177, while Vergil, *Aen.* iv. 511, calls her 'tergemina Hecate.' The goddess was Luna or Cynthia in heaven, Diana on earth, Proserpina in hell.

386. *this hallowed house* Cf. note ll. 389–90.

387. *with broom* Robin Goodfellow was commonly represented with a broom; he was, in one of his aspects, a household spirit, and to use Reginald Scot's words, he 'would supply the office of servants—specially of maids: as to make a fire in the morning, sweep the house, grind mustard and malt, draw water etc.' (*Discovery of Witchcraft*, ch. xxi. p. 436). Cf. note 2. 1. 36–8.

388. *To sweep the dust behind the door* 'a common practice in large old houses, where the doors of halls and galleries are thrown backward and seldom or never shut' (Farmer). But surely Puck was 'sent before' to remedy such slatternly tricks by sweeping the dust *from* behind the door, in preparation for the advent of his king and queen. Cf. *M.W.W.* 5. 5. 43–6:

Cricket, to Windsor chimneys shalt thou leap;
Where fires thou find'st unraked and hearths unswept,
There pinch the maids as blue as bilberry.
Our radiant queen hates sluts and sluttery.

S.D. Q. 'Enter King and Queene of Fairies, with all
their traine.' We take *with rounds of waxen tapers on
their heads* direct from *M.W.W.* 4. 4. 51; v. next note.

389–90. *Through the house...drowsy fire* It is to us
manifest that these words and all that follow down to
l. 421 were written for a performance in 'the great
chamber' of some private house, and that the exit of
the fairies at Oberon's command was arranged in such
a way that they seemed to be departing on their mission
of consecration from chamber to chamber. This being
so, we find no such difficulty, as others have done, in
these two lines. The performance was at night ('The
iron tongue of midnight hath told twelve' l. 361); and
as Theseus and his court left the stage, the candles that
illumined it were extinguished one by one until the only
light that shone was the glow of the embers on the hearth.
It was in this twilight, we believe, that the fairies made
their entry, after Puck's prologue, streaming into the hall,
and kindling their tapers at the hearth as they passed by
it. These tapers, be it noted, were worn on the head, not
carried in the hand, as is clear from the reference to
dancing 'hand in hand' l. 397. We have a scene closely
resembling this in *M.W.W.* 5. 5., where the Fairy-
Queen, like Oberon here, bids the fairies, each crowned
with lighted tapers, dance through Windsor Castle, and
'strew good luck...on every sacred room.' Possibly the
head-dresses for these 'rounds,' which would be fitted
with some sort of metal shield to prevent the wax
running down on to the hair and into the eyes, were
valuable stage-property for which as much employment
would be found as possible. v. pp. 87–8.

399–421. *Now, until the break of day* etc. Q. simply
heads this 'Ob.' F. gives no speech-heading, prints the
whole in italics, and describes it as 'The Song.' Dr Johnson restored it to Oberon, following the Q. He adds:

But where then is the song?—I am afraid it is gone after
many other things of greater value. The truth is that two

songs are lost. The series of the scene is this: after the speech of Puck, Oberon enters, and calls his fairies to a song, which song is apparently wanting in all the copies. Next Titania leads another song, which is indeed lost like the former, though the editors have endeavoured to find it. Then Oberon dismisses his fairies to the despatch of the ceremonies. The songs, I suppose, were lost, because they were not inserted in the players' parts, from which the drama was printed.

This seems to have been generally accepted as the sad truth of the matter, until 1923 when Mr Richmond Noble published his *Shakespeare's Use of Song* in which he claimed that the F. was right in calling 'Now, until the break of day' the song, and that the Q. was also right in assigning it to Oberon; the fact being 'that in the ditty, which the fairies were to take up, Oberon was to lead and presumably to commence solo' (p. 56). It is a simple and an entirely admirable solution of a long-standing problem. We have only one point to add, viz. that the words of both Oberon and Titania had from the beginning contained quite definite instructions that the song was to be sung in this way, though no editor since the days of Shakespeare had ever noticed them. 'And this ditty *after me* sing' says Oberon. Whereupon his Queen replies:

> First rehearse *your song* by rote,
> To each word a warbling note.
> Hand in hand, with fairy grace,
> Will *we sing* and bless this place.

The change from the second person to the first makes it abundantly clear that her bidding to rehearse the song is addressed to Oberon. In short Oberon's 'ditty' and Titania's 'song' are the same, and not two different songs as Johnson imagined. Mr Richmond Noble suggests that the other fairies 'do not join in' with Oberon's song until the third line, and their part would seem to end with 'Shall upon their children be.' Moreover he points

out, as contributory evidence, that it is in just these lines
that the colons occur, colons which 'are musician's stops,
necessary alike for the slow-tripping movement and for
the repetition after Oberon.'

417–18. These lines are accidentally transposed in
Q. Having set up ll. 414 and 415 with 'Euery' and
'And' one above the other, the compositor was perhaps
unconsciously led to repeat the same pattern, so to speak,
with 'Ever' and 'And' two lines lower down. Singer
first suggested the rectification.

421. S.D. Q. 'Exeunt.' It can scarcely be doubted
that the play was meant to end here, with the tripping exit of the fairies and their 'glimmering lights.'
Cf. p. 88. It is significant that the F. omits this
'Exeunt' which suggests a different arrangement, e.g.
that Robin came forward and spoke his epilogue before
the fairy-choir departed.

Epilogue spoken by Puck This is our heading, introduced in order to separate ll. 422–37 from the rest of
the text to which, we believe, they do not rightly belong.
Q. assigns them to 'Robin' and prints them, without
any other heading, immediately after l. 421. Cf.
pp. 87–8.

428. *Gentles, do not reprehend* It was these words
which led Fleay to believe the epilogue was written for
a court performance. Mr W. J. Lawrence (*Times
Literary Supplement*, Dec. 9, 1920) argues that they are
appropriate to the public theatre. If the epilogue was
first written, as we think, for some wedding in the
winter of 1594–5, it was intended for a private performance.

430. *I am* The contracted form 'I'm' is not found
in Shakespeare: it does not follow that he did not wish
it to be so pronounced.

432. *the serpent's tongue* i.e. hisses.

436. *Give me your hands* i.e. your applause.

437. S.D. Q. omits 'exit.'

A NOTE ON THE FOLIO TEXT

In 1619, as we have seen on pp. 77–8, Jaggard produced a reprint of the Fisher Q., which he followed with suspicious exactitude. Apparently, however, the constant occurrence of *Queene* and *Quince* in dialogue, stage-direction and speech-heading, strained the resources of his compositors' type. In any event, the italic *Q* seems to have given out on sig. D1 r. and D2 v., and accordingly the name *Peter* had to be resorted to in place of *Quince*. The fact that the F. also reads *Peter* in this same section of the text is a proof that it was set up from the Q. of 1619 and not from the Fisher Q. of 1600. Another proof is the reappearance in 1623 of nearly all the sixty to seventy misprints first introduced into the text in 1619. When we observe, moreover, that to these transmitted misprints the F. compositors added another sixty to seventy of their own, it will be evident that the F. version cannot claim much textual authority. The misprints in question, most of which occur in the dialogue, belong to the usual order of compositors' errors which we have sufficiently exemplified in the list given in the *Much Ado* volume (pp. 154–56). It is not necessary, therefore, to dwell further upon them here. More interesting are the handful of 'corrections' which the F. introduces into the dialogue, some of them being undoubtedly derived from an agency outside Jaggard's office. And the character of this agency becomes clear directly we turn to the variants which alone give real significance to the F. text, namely the changes in stage-directions and speech-headings.

No doubt the printing-house had its share in these changes. For instance, the F. compositors inadvertently omitted line 3. 2. 344, together of course with the *Exeunt* which should come at the end of it. On the other hand, Q. 1619 supplies a few missing exits in places where the need for them was obvious, and these of course F. takes over. Or consider the little piece of typographical history revealed by the conclusion of Titania's speech at 3. 1. 151–53, in its three forms:

Q. 1600   And I will purge thy mortall groſſeneſſe ſo,
              That thou ſhalt, like an ayery ſpirit goe.
            Peaſe-bloſſome, Cobweb, Moth, and *Muſtard-ſeede?*
              Enter foure Fairyes.

Q. 1619 And I will purge thy mortall groſſeneſſe ſo,
            That thou ſhalt like an ayry ſpirit go.
            Peaſe-bloſſome, Cobweb, Moth, and Muſtard-ſeed.
                  Enter foure Fairies.

F. 1623 And I will purge thy mortall groſſneſſe ſo,
            That thou ſhalt like an airie ſpirit go.
            Enter Peaſe-bloſſome, Cobweb, Moth, Muſtard-
            ſeede, and foure Fairies.

The omission of the question-mark and the italicising of the 'and' in l. 153 by the 1619 compositors are essential links in the chain of corruption, and once again furnish proof that the F. compositors used the 1619 text. It was Furness who first pointed out the origin of this confusion in the F. It was the same editor who first perceived the significance of other F. stage-directions. At 3. 1. 106 the F. supplies *Enter Piramus with the Aſſe head.* 'In all modern editions,' writes Furness, 'the last three words have been changed to "*an* Ass's head," but the prompter of Shakespeare's theatre, knowing well enough that there was among the scanty properties but one Ass-head, inserted in the text "with *the* Asse head"—the only one they had[1].' In other words, though the F. compositors used a copy of the Jaggard Q. of 1619, that copy had itself either served as a prompt-book in the theatre or had been carefully collated with such a prompt-book. An even clearer indication of the prompter's presence is to be found in *Tawyer with a Trumpet before them* which F. prefixes to the entry of Quince's dumb-show at 5. 1. 125; for, as Halliwell discovered[2], Tawyer is the name of an actor, or rather a playhouse servant, who died in 1625 and was described in the sexton's register as 'Mr. Heminges man.' Now it is perfectly obvious that the bulk of the Q. stage-directions, before coming into the hands of the F. compositors, had been amplified, rectified and generally overhauled by some masterful person. The entry of Tawyer with his trumpet and of Bottom with 'the ass-head' tells us who this masterful person was: he was the stage-manager of Shakespeare's company, possibly Heminge himself or his friend Condell, and he made these changes, we cannot doubt, in preparation for some performance of the play between 1600 and 1623. By examining the changes a little more

---

1 *Variorum* edition, pp. xiii–xv.
2 *Outlines,* p. 500.

closely it will be possible, we think, to discover something of the fashion in which they were made and of the kind of performance the stage-manager had in view.

Missing exits have been supplied at 2. 2. 95; 3. 1. 100; 5. 1. 204, 262, and missing entries at 3. 1. 106; 3. 2. 441; 5. 1. 313. A superfluous *Helena* has been omitted at 1. 1. 19. The words *Manet Lyfander and Hermia* have been added to the Q. *Exeunt* at 1. 1. 127, apparently lest it should be supposed that the scene ended at this point. At 3. 1. 82 Q. gives an ambiguous *Exit*, which F. renders *Exit. Pir.* where the double period suggests that the *Pir.* has been added in the margin of Q. Similarly at 5. 1. 107 F. reprints *Enter the Prologue* from Q. and then adds, at the end of the line, an explanatory *Quince*. Again, the entry at the head of 3. 2. runs *Enter King of Fairies, and Robin goodfellow* in Q. and *Enter King of Pharies, folus* in F., which also adds *Enter Pucke* at l. 3. Clearly the Q. direction was not sufficiently exact for the prompter, who has therefore deleted it (as the spelling 'Pharies' demonstrates), written his own version over against it in the margin, and provided Puck with an entry at the right place. Another clarification of the same kind is the translation of *and the rabble* at the head of 4. 2. into *Snout and Starueling*, while in connexion with this last, *Flut.* has been altered to *Staru.* at 4. 2. 3, and 'Snout' substituted for 'Flute' in the dialogue at 5. 1. 155.

Some of the foregoing changes, we have suggested, were made by means of additions in the margin of a copy of the Q. It is possible to go even further, and to show reason for thinking that others were intended to refer to certain pages in the Q. rather than to particular lines. Thus at 3. 2. 416 F. reads *fhifting places*, a direction which though clearly an echo of Demetrius' 'shifting every place' seven lines further on, has no special reference to the line against which it is printed. Turn, however, to Q. 1600, where the line in question falls exactly in the middle of a page which comprises practically all the dialogue concerning Puck's game of blindman's buff with Lysander and Demetrius (sig. F2 r.), and the purpose of the marginal note is not far to seek. The stagebusiness, involving as it did the entry and re-entry of both men, one after the other, to say nothing of still more complicated movements on the part of Puck, would need careful and probably frequent rehearsal. What more natural than that the stage-manager should make a special note in the margin of this critical page in the prompt-book, so that he could turn it up easily whenever he wanted it? In like manner, *Enter Pucke* which F. prints quite incorrectly at 3. 1. 49, whilst retaining the correct Q. *Enter Robin* at 3. 1. 71, may be explained as a jotting, this time written at the top of a Q. page, to remind the manager that Puck should be 'ready' about this time. The misplacing of *Enter Piramus with the Affe head* (3. 1. 106) is to be accounted for in the same way.

The foregoing examples, then, would lead us to suppose that the F. text was derived from a copy of the Q. over which the stage-manager or prompter of the King's Men had worked, freely altering and adding to the stage-directions, and occasionally scribbling signpost notes in the margin. We say 'derived,' because while it is tempting to believe that the F. was printed direct from this quarto prompt-book, it seems more probable that Jaggard took a clean copy and collated it with the one in use at the theatre[1]. If we could establish direct contact between the compositors of 1623 and the prompt-book, it would follow that the prompt-book was a copy of the 1619 Q., and consequently that the performance for which the prompt-book was prepared took place some time between 1619 and 1623. But though we cannot pin the performance down within these narrow limits, we can gather a little more about it by looking at some of the other F. stage-directions.

Already in 1600 the *Dream* was a musical play; in the F. version it becomes noisier if not more musical. We have noted above the heralding of the dumb-show in 5. 1. by Tawyer and his trumpet. Again in obedience to Bottom's request at 4. 1. 29 the F. provides *Muficke Tongs, Rurall Muficke*, a 'scenical direction,' which according to Capell 'is certainly an interpolation of the players,' seeing that

---

[1] One reason for thinking that he did so is that while Q. gives the speech at 5. 1. 44–60 to Theseus alone, F. divides it between .Theseus and Lysander, assigning the 'brief' to the latter and the comments upon it to the former. Now each item of the 'brief' in Q. 1600 is followed by a question-mark, as if it were a query put to some one who replies with the comments, and it looks very probable that it was these queries which suggested the F. arrangement. If so then the theatre prompt-book was almost certainly a copy of Q. 1600 seeing that all the queries but two towards the end of the speech, have been eliminated in Q. 1619.

Titania's hurried attempt to change the conversation 'is a clear exclusion of it.' Further, *Muſick ſtill* (4. 1. 82) seems to be a warning to the musicians not to begin until l. 84. But it is what may be called the sleeping-arrangements of the play that seemed most particularly to engage the theatrical scribe's attention. Thus F. adds *Shee ſleepes* at the end of Titania's lullaby (2. 2. 34), *They ſleepe* at 2. 2. 73, *Awa.* (i.e. Demetrius awakes) at 3. 2. 136, *Bottome wakes* at 4. 1. 198, and *Sleepers Lye ſtill* at 4. 1. 100. This last was a very necessary addition, seeing that the sleepers are to 'start up' at the sound of horns after l. 137 and might therefore easily mistake the horns which announce Theseus at l. 101 for their cue unless great care were observed. Difficulties of another kind occasioned the direction *They ſleepe all the Act*, which the F. prints at the end of Act 3, and which as the most interesting of all the F. additions deserves a special paragraph to itself.

The word 'Act' in this stage-direction is explained as 'interval' by Creizenach (*English Drama*, p. 247 n.), and there can be no reasonable doubt that he is correct. Cotgrave in his French dictionary of 1611 glosses *acte* as 'an Act or pause in a Comedy or Tragedy'; and we find the same meaning given to the word in Marston's *What you will* and Middleton's *Changeling*. Accordingly, in our *Textual Introduction* we claimed the stage-direction as 'an important clue, and one eloquent of the shifts which a curtainless stage imposed upon those who attempted to divide the seamless texture of Shakespeare's dramas' (*Temp.* p. xxxvi). An absurd arrangement which kept the four lovers lying in full view of the audience during the interval for music could hardly have been tolerated by Shakespeare, and we can feel pretty certain that had he been consulted he would have condemned the interval which made such an arrangement necessary. Apart, however, from this, and from the larger question of the introduction of act-divisions into the text of the plays, there is another point to consider. If the King's Men were determined upon their 'act,' why were they forced to leave the sleeping lovers thus exposed while it lasted? Why did they not arrange for them to 'sleep' on the inner-stage, where they could be concealed by the drawing of the traverse when the interval came? An effective answer to these questions would be that no inner-stage was available for the performance of which the F. text is a record. And that this

is the right answer is, we think, borne out by the change
which F. makes in the scenic arrangements for the Mechanicals' play in 5. 1. In the Q. Pyramus and Thisby
clearly die upon the inner-stage, and Moonshine and Lion
draw the traverse by way of 'burying the dead'; in the F.
on the other hand, the dead make way for the Bergomask
by getting up and walking off, and the alteration is effected
by a slight redistribution of parts (cf. notes 5. 1. 347–49,
350). It would seem, therefore, that the F. performance, if
we may so call it, took place not in a public theatre but
at some private house where no inner-stage could be provided. Are we to look for yet another noble wedding as the
occasion of this private performance?

Finally, the stage-direction at the head of 5. 1. runs in
Q. *Enter Thefeus, Hyppolita, and Philoftrate,* and in F.
Enter Thefeus, Hippolita, Egeus and his Lords. Moreover,
wherever Q. reads 'Philostrate' in the dialogue or speech-
headings of this scene, F. substitutes 'Egeus.' The purpose
of the change is perfectly clear: the manager wishes to double
a 'part'; Philostrate has nothing to say except in 5. 1.;
Egeus has nothing to say in 5. 1.; let Egeus therefore take
over Philostrate's speeches in the name of economy and
common sense! The alteration was all in the direction of
theatrical efficiency; whether it was dramatically appropriate is another matter.

The nature and object of the F. variants in stage-directions and speech-headings are now clear; and it should not
be necessary to argue that Shakespeare himself had nothing
whatever to do with them. Even less easy is it to imagine
him in any way responsible for the F. 'corrections' in the
dialogue. Here is a list of those which are unlikely to be
due to the compositors: 2. 2. 112 nature her fhewes < nature
fhewes; 3. 2. 220 your paffionate words < your words;
3. 2. 257 No, no, Sir < No, no: heele; 4. 1. 191–92 *om.* Are
you fure That we are awake?; 5. 1. 34 our < or; 5. 1. 190
knit vp in thee < knit now againe; 5. 1. 205 the morall
downe < the Moon vfed. These variants are almost certainly
due to the scribe who gave us the F. stage-directions. Some
of them are good, some indifferent, and some definitely bad;
but all are assuredly guesses.

THE STAGE-HISTORY OF
A MIDSUMMER-NIGHT'S DREAM

Meres mentions *A Midsummer-Night's Dream* in *Palladis Tamia* (1598). The title-page of the quarto of 1600 says that it had been publicly acted by the Lord Chamberlain's servants. In 1624, a Protestant writer, John Gee, mentions in his book, *New Shreds of the Old Snare*, the comedy of '*Piramus and Thisbe*, where one comes in with a Lanthorne and Acts *Mooneshine*.' In his *Works*, published in 1630, John Taylor, the water-poet, calls the play by its true name, and quotes the prologue to the clowns' tragedy (Address to Nobody, prefixed to *Sir Gregory Nonsence his Newes from No Place*). Evidently, the play, or some part of it, held the stage in the reigns of James I and Charles I; but the title given to it by Gee might suggest that already the popularity of the clowns had led to their being separated from the comedy, as they have been since in a hundred theatres, and in innumerable school speech-days. They were certainly so separated after the closing of the theatres in 1642. Their rehearsal and performance were turned, as Francis Kirkman records in *The Wits*, into one of the 'humours and pieces of Plays, which... were only allowed us, and that but by stealth too, and under pretence of Rope-dancing, or the like.' This 'droll,' called *The Merry Conceited Humors of Bottom the Weaver*, was published separately by Kirkman and Marsh in 1661, and included by Kirkman in *The Wits* in 1673. The characters are the clowns, Oberon and Titania (who are 'doubled' with 'the Duke and Dutchess') and 'Pugg.' It is pure Shakespeare.

The droll was popular; the comedy as a whole did not suit the taste of the Restoration. It was one of the

Shakespeare plays chosen by Killigrew for the King's company when he and D'Avenant divided the repertory; but only one performance of it under his management is recorded: that which Pepys saw at the theatre in Vere-street on September 29, 1662: 'To the King's Theatre, where we saw "Midsummer's Night's Dream," which I had never seen before, nor shall ever again, for it is the most insipid ridiculous play that ever I saw in my life.' True, it offered him 'some good dancing and some handsome women, which was all my pleasure'; and his words imply that this was not the first time that it had been given since acting began again; but the production was probably simple and without the allure of spectacle. It was not till later in the seventeenth century that the theatre, having elaborated its scenic devices and created a taste for display, discovered that some of Shakespeare's comedies made good raw material for scenes, machines and music. In 1692 Betterton produced at the Queen's Theatre (formerly called Dorset Garden, and famous under D'Avenant for spectacle) an operatic and spectacu-lar piece, *The Fairy Queen* (published by Tonson in 1692), founded upon Shakespeare's play. The course of the comedy was not much altered, except that Hippolyta was left out, and the clowns' play was trans-ferred to the third act and performed in the wood. The object of this change was doubtless to leave more room in the last act for the spectacle, of which each act had one and the last act the most sumptuous, with a chorus of Chineses, a dance of six monkeys, a Chinese garden, and what not. Shakespeare's verse was not much changed, except in Theseus's speech on Imagination; and music by Henry Purcell was among the attractions of what seems to have been Betterton's supreme achievement in this kind of thing. 'The Court and Town,' says Downes, the prompter, 'were wonderfully satisfy'd with it; but the Expences in setting it out being so great, the Com-pany got little by it.' That story has been heard in the theatre since. By 1703 *The Fairy Queen* had shrunk to be a one-act interlude in a concert.

Betterton's example was soon followed and outdone. During more than a century, the comedy was frequently and ruthlessly adapted into an opera. John Rich, carrying on at Lincoln's Inn Fields the tradition of spectacle and music, produced there, on October 19, 1716, as an after-piece to Thomas Jevon's farce, *The Devil of a Wife*, a work by Richard Leveridge, entitled *The Comick Masque of Pyramus and Thisbe* (published in 1716). Leveridge did much what the droll had done before. He took the clowns and left out the lovers; and he is scarcely to be blamed, seeing that his little masque was 'composed in the high stile of Italy'; that is, as a jest at the craze for Italian opera. Three musicians, Semi-breve, Crochet and Gamut, attend a rehearsal of the clowns' play and use up some of the Athenians' com-ments, adding many all their own.   Everyone sings, including the lion. With Spiller as Bottom (replaced by Leveridge himself when Bottom assumed the singing part of Pyramus), the mock opera was played more than once as an after-piece to *Timon of Athens*, and at least once after *The Gamester*. At Drury Lane on January 9, 1723, the clowns' play, pretty much as Shakespeare wrote it, was pitchforked by Charles Johnson into *Love in a Forest*, his version of *As You Like It*, for the amusement of the banished Duke and his fellows in the forest. On January 25, 1745, Covent Garden pro-duced, as an after-piece to *The Miser*, an enlarged version by the German musician, John Frederick Lampe, of Leveridge's mock opera, with many new songs, Beard playing Pyramus and Mrs Lampe Thisbe. For ten years this Leveridge-Lampe travesty was all that the stage knew of *A Midsummer-Night's Dream*. They were acting it as late as 1754.

Then, in February, 1755, a grand new perversion of the play was presented by Garrick at Drury Lane. It was called *The Fairies* (published 1755), and the

compiler (possibly Garrick himself) turned the tables
on the previous adapters by leaving out the clowns and
with them, of course, the ass's head, thereby obscuring
the story of Oberon and Titania. The prologue attributed the play to 'Signor Shakespearelli'; and on seeing
in the cast the names of Signor Curioni as Lysander
and Signora Passerini as Hermia we do not need to be
assured that this 'blessed exhibition,' as Tate Wilkinson
called it, was but another opera. The music was chiefly
by Smith. The songs were taken from many sources,
including Shakespeare's other plays, Dryden, and Milton.
The dialogue was cut freely, though but little rewritten.
Beard, a famous singer, was the Theseus, and the fairies
were all played by children. Four performances are
recorded, and the whole run was estimated at nine. But
Garrick's Drury Lane had not done with *A Midsummer-
Night's Dream*. During Garrick's absence abroad, a
piece bearing that title was performed on its stage in
November, 1763 (printed 1763). Whether Garrick
himself, or his deputy, the elder Colman, were responsible for it—and each blamed it on the other—it was
a dead failure, and was performed no more than once.
It was an opera, of course, with the clowns this time
partially restored, though most of their play was left out;
and with Yates for Bottom, Baddeley for Flute, and
Parsons for Starveling, that part of it at least must have
been well acted and sung. Colman saved what he could
of it by cutting out Theseus and Hippolyta and the lovers
(though Miss Young had played Hermia and Mrs Vin-
cent Helena) and making the opera into an after-piece,
which he called *A Fairy-Tale*. This proved a useful
little stop-gap. It is found on the stage of Drury Lane
as late as 1768, and again at the Haymarket in the
summer of 1777, when it was first printed. The clowns'
play is left out altogether, and though Bottom is lured
off by Puck there is no mention of his wearing the ass's
head when he returns—his natural clownishness being
sufficient, it must be presumed, to make Titania's

passion ridiculous. The last news of the play in the eighteenth century is from Bath, where in March, 1794, Blisset plays Bottom in a *Comical Tragedy of Pyramus and Thisbe*, and a fortnight or so later Elliston plays Bottom in *A Midsummer-Night's Dream*. What relation this piece or these pieces bore to Shakespeare's work there is no telling now.

The eighteenth century had evidently been puzzled about the unity and proportions of a play composed of three pretty distinct elements: fairies, human lovers and clowns. It had picked and chosen, generally the clowns. The nineteenth century very soon shows someone at least trying to see the play as a whole, instead of snippeting it into after-pieces and burlesques. In January, 1816, John Philip Kemble, nearing the end of his reign at Covent Garden, produced (but did not act in) a version by Frederic Reynolds (printed 1816)—an operatic version still, with music by Henry Bishop, supplemented with songs by Arne and Smith. Thus did Reynolds enter on his evil, successful career of making operas out of Shakespeare. 'Not acted 50 years,' says the bill: 'not acted two hundred years, and not yet to be acted' would have been nearer the mark. John Kemble's production not only borrowed from the two Drury Lane versions: it went back to Betterton by misplacing the clowns' play so as to leave room in the last act for a display, not indeed of Chineses and monkeys, but of the victories of Theseus. The scenery and pageantry are recorded as very elaborate and splendid; and with Liston as Bottom, Emery as Quince, Miss Stephens as Hermia, Miss Foote as Helena, Miss Sally Booth as Puck and Mrs Faucit as Titania, the acting ought to have been very good. But by 1816 certain people had discovered that Shakespeare knew his job as playwright better than to deserve such alteration; and one of them, Hazlitt, was moved to a famous outburst. In *The Examiner* of January 21, 1816, he wrote: 'All that is fine in the play, was lost in the representation. The spirit was evaporated, the genius was fled; but the spectacle was fine: it was that which saved the play. Oh, ye scene-shifters, ye scene-painters, ye machinists and dressmakers, ye manufacturers of moon and stars that give no light, ye musical composers, ye men in the orchestra, fiddlers and trumpeters and players on the double drum and loud bassoon, rejoice! This is your triumph; it is not ours: and ye full-grown, well-fed, substantial, real fairies,...we shall remember you: we shall believe no more in the existence of your fantastic tribe....All that was good in this piece (except the scenery) was Mr Liston's Bottom.' He sums up with a principle favoured in his time: 'Poetry and the stage do not agree together....The *ideal* has no place upon the stage, which is a picture without perspective; every thing there is in the foreground. That which is merely an airy shape, a dream, a passing thought, immediately becomes an unmanageable reality.'

The theatre listened to Hazlitt no more than it has listened to any critic. He had been in his grave two years when, forgetting even John Kemble's attempt to give the play as a whole, Covent Garden squeezed into a musical version of *All's Well That Ends Well* a masque called *Oberon and Robin Goodfellow*; and a year later, in November, 1833, Alfred Bunn serves up at Drury Lane an after-piece in two acts, with music which Professor Odell describes as 'compiled from all the Midsummer Night's Dreams that had disgraced the stage from Garrick to Reynolds.' A decade after Hazlitt's death, however, some of his, or Coleridge's, or Lamb's, ideas about Shakespeare as poet and playwright had penetrated into the theatre; and, to judge from contemporary accounts, Hazlitt himself might have approved the production of *A Midsummer-Night's Dream* given by Mme Vestris and Charles Mathews as a play, not an opera, in November, 1840, during their second season at Covent Garden. J. R. Planché, who made the version for them, kept closely to Shakespeare. He used nothing that was not in Shakespeare's original: he even saw that Shakespeare's own ending to the play made a better final scene for it than any pageant of them all. Some attempt at archaeological accuracy in the dresses seems to have resulted, at any rate, in beauty; the scenery, by the Grieves, aiming also, in its degree, at fidelity to ancient Athens, was much admired; and the music, composed and selected by T. Cooke, included 'Mendelssohn's celebrated overture.'

Samuel Phelps's production at Sadler's Wells in October, 1853, would have come yet nearer than that of the pioneer Mme Vestris to convincing Hazlitt that poetry and the stage might agree together, and that a stage moon might give light. From the accounts left by Henry Morley and others, this may be concluded to be the most Shakespearian production that had ever been given; and at least it was not surpassed in the nineteenth century. Bottom was one of Phelps's best parts, and he played it again in September, 1870, at the Queen's Theatre, Long Acre. But better even than the acting of Phelps and of his capable, undistinguished company at Sadler's Wells was the dream-like, fairy-like atmosphere of the whole production. When Charles Kean staged the comedy at the Princess's Theatre in October, 1856, with a cast that included neither himself nor his wife, but gave Bottom to Harley and Puck to a child of eight named Ellen Terry, he lost the dream and the fairy feeling. He cut Shakespeare down a good deal to make room for spectacle, some of which (especially that obvious absurdity, a shadow-dance by fairies) was severely blamed by good critics. The whole was found wanting in poetry, no matter what its archaeological pretensions and its splendour. And this fault of missing the poetry may be charged against some subsequent productions. There have been a good many in the last three or four decades, all attempting, not all succeeding, to get back to Shakespeare's own idea of the unity and the proportions of his play. Mr F. R. Benson gave it in London in 1889 and 1890. Daly gave it—only moderately altered—at Daly's Theatre in 1895, with Miss Ada Rehan not at her most interesting as Helena. Tree very sumptuously gave it at Her Majesty's Theatre in 1900; and again in 1911, when Mr Arthur Bourchier replaced him in the part of Bottom and the poetry of the enchanted wood was sought by means of live rabbits on the stage. In contrast with this were the sound, unextravagant production by Mr Oscar Asche at the Adelphi in 1905; and the pretty version of Mr Oscar Barrett at the Crystal Palace in 1896. In 1908 the Oxford University Dramatic Society essayed it; in 1916 the boys of Bradfield College gave it freshly and pleasantly in their Gray Pit, or Greek theatre.

In 1914 the twentieth century brought its ideas of the production of Shakespeare to bear on the comedy that had puzzled the eighteenth and mainly defeated the nineteenth. Those ideas include the abandonment of elaborate staging and of archaeological accuracy. By means of an 'apron-stage,' more or less corresponding to the Shakespearian platform-stage, and of simple, easily changed scenery, they attempt almost continuous performance of the complete text; and they replace archaeology with a distinct poetic or 'atmospheric' convention for each play. A capital instance of these aims was given by Mr Granville Barker's production of *A Midsummer-Night's Dream* on the temporary 'apron-stage' of the Savoy Theatre. Details in the production were hotly attacked, and nothing in it more hotly than Mr Norman Wilkinson's scenery and costumes, in which the fairies were remarkable for their Oriental style and their gilded faces—Eastern creatures, and made of moonshine. There was some freakishness about it all; but the production achieved, within its rather strange convention of style, its purpose, which was to preserve the proportions of Shakespeare's play as he left them, and to steep the whole in the strangeness of moonlight and of dream. The play was staged on similar lines at the Kingsway Theatre in November, 1923.

In December, 1920, James Bernard Fagan opened his management of the Court Theatre with this play,

Oberon by Mary Gray, and Titania by Elizabeth Irving (daughter of H. B. Irving and grand-daughter of Sir Henry). The music was by John Greenwood. In December, 1924, there was a sumptuous revival at Drury Láne, with Hay Petrie as Puck and ballets by Michel Fokine. From 1933 onwards the comedy has been a regular feature of the summer productions of the Open Air Theatre in the Regent's Park, where, as in nearly all other productions, the music used is Mendelssohn's.

On October 7, 1922, the Motion Picture Directors Association, of America, produced in the Hollywood Bowl a play (not a motion picture) entitled *Midsummer Night's Dream*. Some diverting particulars of the not strictly Shakespearian cast, which included Tom Mix and his pony Tony, may be found in Hazelton Spencer's *Shakespeare Improved*, p. 324.

Twelve years later, in September, 1934, another production of *A Midsummer Night's Dream* on a great scale was seen in the same spot. The producer was Max Reinhardt. Between 1905, when he first produced this play in Berlin, and April, 1933, when the Nazi rule dispensed with his services, Reinhardt had given four different productions of the play in Germany and one at Salzburg. In May, 1933, he gave a performance of it at Florence, and in the following month produced the play for the Oxford University Dramatic Society, which acted it in the open air in the grounds of Southbank, Headington. The Hollywood production of September, 1934, was the basis of the film that was seen in London in 1935.   HAROLD CHILD.

A note on the Sources

See p. xvii above; Mr Walter de la Mare's Introduction to *A Midsummer Night's Dream* (The Scholar's Library), Macmillan and Co. 1935, reprinted in *Pleasures and Speculations*, 1940; and 'Variations on the theme of *A Midsummer Night's Dream*' by J. D. W. in *Tribute to Walter de la Mare on his 75th Birthday*, 1948.

GLOSSARY

Note. Where a pun or quibble is intended, the meanings are distinguished as (*a*) and (*b*)

ABRIDGMENT, usually explained as 'something to shorten or while away the time'; but O.E.D. queries this. A more likely interpretation would be 'a short, or shortened, play for an evening's entertainment at court'; 5. 1. 39

ABY, pay the penalty for; 3. 2. 175

ADAMANT, a fabulous rock or stone to which were ascribed properties both of the diamond or other hard gems and of the loadstone or magnet (v. O.E.D.); 2. 1. 195

ADDRESSED, ready; 5. 1. 106

ADMIRABLE, wonderful; 5. 1. 27

ADVANCE, reveal (cf. O.E.D., 6); 3. 2. 128

AFTER-SUPPER, variously interpreted as (i) dessert at the end of supper, and (ii) a rere-supper or second supper late at night. The context seems to point to (i), since the court would hardly wait up three hours after a rere-supper; 5. 1. 34.

AGGRAVATE, lit. exaggerate. Bottom, of course, means the opposite; 1. 2. 75

ALONE, unique, unequalled (cf. *Gent.* 2. 4. 165); 3. 2. 119

ANTIC, grotesque (the world also carries with it a suggestion of 'antique'); 5. 1. 3

ANTIPODES, the people who dwell on the other side of the earth; 3. 2. 55

APPROVE, test, try; 2. 2. 76

APRICOCK, obs. form of 'apricot'; 3. 1. 157

ARGUMENT, theme for jest or scorn; 3. 2. 242

ART, magic art; 1. 1. 192; 2. 2. 112

ARTIFICIAL, skilled in art; 'like two artificial gods'=like two skilful creators; 3. 2. 203

AURORA'S HARBINGER, Venus Phosphor, the morning-star (cf. *fairy time*); 3. 2. 380

BADGE, the hall-mark (as we should say). Lit.=the mark worn by retainers (cf. *Temp.* 5. 1. 268–69 'Mark but the badges of these men, my lords, Then say if they be true'); 3. 2. 127

BARM, yeast; 2. 1. 38

BATED, excepted; 1. 1. 190

BAY, lit. 'to bark at,' hence 'to hunt with a pack of barking hounds,' and finally the notion of barking has disappeared in 'to bring to bay,' v. O.E.D.; 4. 1. 112.

BERGOMASK, a dance of clowns or rustics. The inhabitants of Bergamo, a province in the state of Venice, were considered particularly rustic in speech and manners; 5. 1. 352–3

BESHREW, evil befall, mischief take; 2. 2. 62

BETEEM, grant, vouchsafe. Possibly Shakespeare also had in mind 'teem'=pour (O.E.D. quotes 'beteem'=pour from, 1618); 1. 1. 131

BOND, (a) signed contract, (b) fetter; 3. 2. 267

BOTTLE, a bundle of hay or straw, the feed prescribed for a horse by Elizabethan horse-keepers (*Sh. Eng.* i. 350). This word, which is etymologically quite distinct from 'bottle' meaning a vessel, is still found in the proverb 'to look for a needle in a bottle of hay'; 4. 1. 33

BOTTOM, the core of the skein upon which a weaver wound his wool (cf. *Gent.* 3. 2. 53); 1. 2. 16 etc.

BRIEF, list, summary; 5. 1. 42

BULLY, a term of endearment meaning 'gallant, fine fellow,' etc.; 3. 1. 7; 4. 2. 18

BY'R LAKIN, a vulgar form of 'By our Lady'; 3. 1. 12

CANKER-BLOSSOM, a worm that cankers a blossom; 3. 2. 282

CAPACITY, 'to my c.'=as I understand things; 5. 1. 105

CAROL, orig. 'a ring-dance with song,' hence 'any kind of song sung at times of festival'; 2. 1. 102

CARRY, conquer; 5. 1. 231

CAVALERY, i.e. Cavaliero, a form of address meaning 'gallant, gentleman' (cf. *M.W.W.* 2. 3. 68 'Cavaliero Slender'); 4. 1. 22

CHEER, countenance; 3. 2. 96

CHIDING, brawling or angry noise (especially of hounds); 4. 1. 114

CHILDING, breeding, fruitful, pregnant; 2. 1. 112

CHOUGH, jackdaw; 3. 2. 21

CLOSE, secluded, secret; 3. 2. 7

COIL, fuss, bother; 3. 2. 339

COLLIED, begrimed, murky; 1.1.145

COMPANION, fellow (contemptuous); 1. 1. 15

CON, commit to memory; 1. 2. 93

CONDOLE, grieve, lament. Shakespeare considered this word ridiculous; 1. 2. 23, 37

CONFEDERACY, conspiracy; 3. 2. 192

CONFERENCE, conversation, talk (less formal and more general than the mod. meaning); 2. 2. 54

CONTINENTS, i.e. the banks which should contain them; 2. 1. 92

CORIN and Phillida are the traditional names of lovers in pastoral poetry; 2. 1. 66, 68

COURAGEOUS. Quince means 'brave'; 4. 2. 24

COY, pat, caress; 4. 1. 2

CRAZÉD, unsound, flawed; 1. 1. 92

CRY, a pack of hounds; 4. 1. 123

CUE, v. *part*; 3. 1. 71, 95, 96

CURST, cross, ill-tempered, shrewish; 3. 2. 300, 341, 439

CURTSY, bow; 4. 1. 20

DAPHNE, the damsel who fleeing from Apollo's importunities was changed into a laurel at her own request (Ovid, *Met.* i. 452 et sqq.); 2. 1. 231

DARKLING, in the dark; 2. 2. 94

DEAD, deadly pale (cf. *Oth.* 2. 3. 177 'Honest Iago, that look'st dead with grieving'); 3. 2. 57

DEFECT, Bottom's blunder for 'effect'; 3. 1. 35

DEVICE, a play or masque written for private representation (cf. *L.L.L.* 5. 2. 663; *Tim.* 1. 2. 155); 5. 1. 50

DEWLAP, a pendulous fold of skin on the throat; 2. 1. 50; 4. 1. 121

DISCHARGE, act, perform, play a part (apparently a technical term of the theatre; cf. *Temp.* 2. 1. 249–51 'to perform an act,/ Whereof what's past is prologue; what to come,/In yours and my discharge'); 1. 2. 85; 4. 2. 8; 5. 1. 359

DISFIGURE, Quince's blunder for 'figure,' i.e. represent; 3. 1. 55

DISSOLVE, (*a*) break faith or troth, (*b*) melt; 1. 1. 245

DISTEMPERATURE, climatic inclemency or unwholesomeness. The word 'temperature' at this period comprised all atmospheric conditions; 2. 1. 106

DOTAGE, infatuation; 4. 1. 46

DOUBLE TONGUE, forked tongue; 2. 2. 9

DOWAGER, a widow with a 'dowage' or jointure charged upon an estate; 1. 1. 5

EGLANTINE, sweet-briar; 2. 1. 252

EIGHT AND SIX, i.e. alternate lines of eight and six syllables, a common ballad metre: 'eight and eight,' which Bottom prefers, was another very common measure in popular verse; 3. 1. 22

ENFORCÉD, violated; 3. 1. 191

ERCLES, Bottom's pronunciation of 'Hercules,' whom he classes among the tyrants; 1. 2. 25, 36

EXPOSITION, Bottom's blunder for 'disposition'; 4. 1. 38

EXTORT, torture; 3. 2. 160

EYNE, an old plur. of 'eyes,' rarely used by the Elizabethans except for rhyming purposes; 1. 1. 242; 5. 1. 176

FAINT, prob. 'pale' not 'faint-scented' (cf. *Wint.* 4. 4. 122; *Cym.* 4. 2. 221); 1. 1. 215

FAIRY TIME, 'begins after midnight and closes at the rising of the morning star' (*Sh. Eng.* i. 536) or a little longer (cf. 3. 2. 388–93); 5. 1. 362

FANCY, (i) love, affectation; 1. 1. 155; 2. 1. 164; 3. 2. 96; 4. 1. 162; (ii) imagination, fantasy ('fancy' was orig. a contraction of 'fantasy'); 5. 1. 25

FANTASY, extravagant fancy; 1. 1. 32; 2. 1. 258; 5. 1. 5

FAVOUR, lit. good-will, (i) something given or worn as a mark of affection or good-will, e.g. a love-token, ribbon, jewel, etc.; 2. 1. 12; 4. 1. 48; (ii) charm of face, good looks; 1. 1. 186

FELL, angry, cruel; 2. 1. 20; 5. 1. 222, 282

FIERCE, wild, excessive; 4. 1. 68

FLEWED, i.e. with 'flews,' the large chaps of a deep-mouthed hound; 4. 1. 119

FORDONE, tired out (cf. mod. slang 'done up'); 5. 1. 372

FORESTER. O.E.D. quotes under 1598 Manwood, *Lawes Forest*, 'A Forester is an officier of a forest of the King (or of another man) that is sworne to preserue the Vert and Venison of the same forest, and to attend upon the wild beasts within his Bailiwick, and to attach offendors there'; 4. 1. 102

FRENCH CROWN, (*a*) the 'écu,' a French gold coin, (*b*) the baldness produced by the 'French disease,' i.e. syphilis; 1. 2. 87, 89

GAUD, toy, trinket (contemptuous); 1. 1. 33; 4. 1. 166

GLANCE AT, cast reflections upon (cf. *Errors*, 5. 1. 66; *Jul. Caes.* 1. 2. 323); 2. 1. 75

GOSSIP, lit. 'a sponsor to a child,' hence 'the familiar friend of a village woman,' hence again 'a talkative person'; 2. 1. 47

GOVERNMENT, the regulation of a musical instrument by means of its stops (cf. *Ham.* 3. 2. 372 'govern these ventages with your fingers and thumb,' etc.); 5. 1. 123

GRIFFIN, a fabulous monster with the head of an eagle and the body of a lion; 2. 1. 232

GRISLY, terrible to behold; 5. 1. 138

GROW TO A POINT, i.e. come to the point. Edd. have questioned this meaning, but cf. *Epitome* (Marprelate Tracts, ed. Pierce, p. 120), 'Alas poor Bishops! you would fain be hidden in a net, I perceive. I will grow to a point with you'; 1. 2. 10

HARBINGER, orig. one who provides or procures lodgings, hence one who preceded a great man on a journey to procure him lodgings, and hence again a forerunner; 3. 2. 380

HECATE (the triple). The goddess was Diana on earth, Phoebe in the heavens and Hecate in the underworld; 5. 1. 382

HEMPEN HOME-SPUN, 'homespun cloth made of hemp; hence one clad in such cloth, one of rustic or coarse manners' O.E.D.; 3. 1. 72

HENCHMAN, 'a squire or page of honour to a prince or great man, who walked or rode beside him in processions, progresses, marches, etc.' O.E.D.; 2. 1. 121

HIGHT, is called (a Spenserian word, burlesqued again by Shakespeare in *L.L.L.*); 5. 1. 138

HOBGOBLIN. 'Hob' was a variation of 'Robert' or 'Robin'; hence 'Hobgoblin' was equivalent to 'Robin Goodfellow'; 2. 1. 40

HOLD, OR CUT BOW-STRINGS, an archer's expression, not yet satisfactorily explained. *Sh. Eng.* (ii. 380*n*.) has no doubt that it implies 'come rain, hail or shine'; Chambers believes it means 'Keep your promises or give up the play'; 1. 2. 103

HOLD UP (the jest), i.e. keep up the joke (cf. *M.W.W.* 5. 5. 102); 3. 2. 239

HUMOUR, disposition, inclination; 1. 2. 24

IMBRUE, lit. to stain with blood, hence to pierce so as to cause blood; 5. 1. 343

IMMEDIATELY, exactly, precisely; 1. 1. 45

IMPEACH, discredit, cast imputations upon; 2. 1. 214

INCREASE, crops, vegetable products (cf. *Psalm* 67. 6; *Son.* 97 'The teeming autumn, big with rich increase'); 2. 1. 114

INJURIOUS, insulting; 3. 2. 195

INJURY, insult; 2. 1. 147

INTEND, offer; 3. 2. 333

INTERLUDE, a short play, generally written for performance in some great man's banqueting-hall (cf. E. K. Chambers, *Med. Stage*, ii. 183); 1. 2. 5; 5. 1. 154

JANGLING, altercation, wrangling; 3. 2. 353

JEALOUSY, suspicion; 4. 1. 143

JEW, probably a playful diminutive of 'juvenal' q.v.; 3. 1. 90

JUGGLER, deceiver, trickster; 3. 2. 282

JUVENAL, i.e. young fellow (a quibble upon 'juvenile': cf. *L.L.L.* G. 'Juvenal'); 3. 1. 90

KNOT-GRASS, the 'Polygonum avi-
culare' or common knot-grass,
a well-known weed, low-creep-
ing with intricately branched
stems which catch the feet, and
very tenacious and difficult to
eradicate. 'An infusion of it was
formerly supposed to stunt the
growth' O.E.D.; 3. 2. 329

LATCH, moisten (v. O.E.D. 'leach'
vb.²); 3. 2. 36
LIVERY, dress, distinctive garb;
1. 1. 70; 2. 1. 113
LOB, clown, lout, lubber (cf.
L'Allegro, 110); 2. 1. 16
LODE-STAR, i.e. the star which
shows the 'lode' or way, and
upon which the sailor's gaze and
hopes are fixed; 1. 1. 183
LOVE-IN-IDLENESS, (*a*) the hearts-
ease, the pansy, (*b*) love without
serious intention (cf. O.E.D.
'idleness' 2, 3); 2. 1. 168
LOVES (of all), a phrase of strong
entreaty (cf. *M.W.W.* 2. 2.
107); 2. 2. 162

MAKING, build, make, personal
appearance; 2. 1. 32
MARGENT, margin; 2. 1. 85
MARSHAL, an officer in a palace or
nobleman's house, charged with
the arrangement of ceremonies
and the presentation of guests;
2. 2. 128
MAZES (in the green), intricate
labyrinths marked out on the
grass and kept fresh by the tread
of boys' feet; 2. 1. 99
MEAN, (*a*) lament for the dead,
(*b*) lodge a formal complaint (the
'videlicet' suggests a side-glance
at this legal sense); 5. 1. 322
MECHANICALS, artisans, mechanics;
3. 2. 9

MEW, cage, up. A term from
falconry; lit. a 'mew' was the
cage where the hawk was kept
during the period of moulting or
'mewing'; 1. 1. 71
MIGHT, 'takes it in might, not
merit,' i.e. values it for the
effort expended rather than for
the skill shown; 5. 1. 92
MIMIC, buffoon, burlesque player,
a contemptuous term for actors
in general; 3. 2. 19
MINIMUS, 'a creature of the smallest size' O.E.D. It is, of course,
the Lat. superlative used as a
substantive; 3. 2. 329
MISGRAFFÉD, ill-grafted together,
badly matched; 1. 1. 137
MISPRISION, mistake; 3. 2. 90
MISPRIZED, mistaken; 3. 2. 74
MOMENTANY, a very common alternative to 'momentary' at this
period (cf. Lat. 'momentaneus'
and 'momentarius'); 1. 1. 143
MOTH, mote. Cf. *L.L.L.* 4. 3. 158
(note); 3. 1. 153, etc.
MURRION, disease of cattle (generally spelt 'murrain'); 2. 1. 97

NEAF, fist; 4. 1. 19
NEEZE, sneeze (of which word it is
a variant form); 2. 1. 56
NIGHT-RULE, revels; 3. 2. 5
NINE MEN'S MORRIS, or Merels, 'a
game for two players or parties,
each of whom had the same
number of pebbles, disks, pegs
or pins. It was known as Nine
Men's Morris, Fivepenny Morris, and Three Men's Morris,
according to the number of
"men" used. The usual form of
the diagram upon which it is
played is a square with one or
more squares inside it. The pegs
or stones placed at set points

are moved by one side so as
to take up the men of the other.
...In the open-air form of the
game the squares are made in
the turf with knives' (*Sh. Eng.*
ii. 467). Obviously a game
not unlike hop-scotch; 2. 1. 98

NOLL, noddle, head. A jocular or
contemptuous term; 3. 2. 17

OBSCENELY. Bottom, like Costard
(*L.L.L.* 4. 1. 142), appears to
think that this word is connected with 'seen' and means
'openly, clearly, so as to be seen';
1. 2. 100

OBSERVATION, observance (cf. 'observe the rite of May' 4. 1.
131-2); 4. 1. 103

OES, small circles or spots, spangles
(cf. *L.L.L.* G. 'O'); 3. 2. 188

ORANGE-TAWNY, deep or dark yellow
(v. *tawny*); 1. 2. 86; 3. 1. 120

ORBS UPON THE GREEN, fairy-rings
(cf. *Temp.* 5. 1. 37); 2. 1. 9

ORIENT PEARL, a pearl from the
Indian seas, more beautiful than
those found in European mus-
sels; hence, a brilliant or precious pearl; 4. 1. 53

OUNCE, lynx; 2. 2. 38

OUSEL, blackbird; 3. 1. 119

OVERFLOWN, overwhelmed (as by
a flood); 4. 1. 16

O'ER-SHOES (to be), a common expression for reckless deter-
mination (cf. *Gent.* G. 'over-
shoes'); 3. 2. 48

OVERWATCH, sit up too late at
night; 5. 1. 364

OWE (adj.), own (an archaic or pro-
vincial form, v. O.E.D. 'own'
a); 3. 1. 142

OWE (vb.), own; 2. 2. 87

PAIN, trouble; 5. 1. 80

PARK, 'over park, over pale'=over
enclosed private property: 'park'
lit. means an enclosure for the
preservation of game, and 'pale'
any piece of ground surrounded
by a fence; the implication is
that all land is 'common' to the
fairies; 2. 1. 4

PARLOUS, a syncopated form of
'perilous'; 3. 1. 12

PART, a player's 'part' comprised
all his speeches written out on
strips of paper. It included the
'cues' which were the final
words of speeches preceding his
own, and served him as signals
when to come in; 1. 2. 17, etc.

PARTITION, (*a*) wall, (*b*) section of
a learned book (v. O.E.D. 4*a*);
5. 1. 166

PAT (adv.), just right; 3. 1. 2

PATCH, fool, clown; 3. 2. 9

PATCHED FOOL, in reference to the
fool's garb; 4. 1. 210

PATENT, privilege; 1. 1. 80

PAVÉD FOUNTAIN, i.e. 'a clear
fountain with a pebbly bottom'
E. K. Chambers; 2. 1. 84

PELTING, petty, paltry; 2. 1. 91

PENSIONER, a reference to the fifty
gentlemen-pensioners or royal
body-guard of Queen Elizabeth,
who were magnificently dressed
in uniforms adorned with gold
lace and jewels (cf. 'in their gold
coats...rubies'); 2. 1. 10

PERT, lively, sprightly; 1. 1. 13

PHIBBUS, i.e. Phoebus, the sun-
god; 1. 2. 31

PHILLIDA, v. *Corin*; 2. 1. 68

PHILOMELE, the classical name for
the nightingale; 2. 2. 13, 25

PLAIN-SONG, a term orig. applied
to simple ecclesiastical chants,
generally in a minor key. As
E. K. Chambers says, this 'un-

varying traditional melody' was peculiarly apt to a metaphor drawn from the cuckoo's monotonous song in a minor third; 3. 1. 125

POINT, (i) summit; 2. 2. 127; (ii) 'stand upon points' = (a) bother about trifles, (b) mind his stops; 5. 1. 118

PREFER, recommend, select for consideration; 4. 2. 34

PREPOST'ROUSLY, contrary to nature, perversely; 3. 2. 121

PRESENT, act, perform a part, represent; 3. 1. 56; 3. 2. 14; 5. 1. 130, 135, 155, 237, 242

PRINCESS (of pure white), i.e. of sovereign whiteness; 3. 2. 144

PRIVILEGE, protection, lit. right of immunity; 2. 1. 220

PURPLE-IN-GRAIN, fast-dyed purple or scarlet; 1. 2. 86

QUAINT, (i) cunning, ingenious; 2. 1. 99; (ii) pretty, dainty; 2. 2. 7

QUELL, destroy, kill; 5. 1. 285

QUERN, hand-mill for grinding corn; 2. 1. 36

QUILL, pipe (a reference to the shrill note of the wren); 3. 1. 122

RECORDER, a vertical flute with a whistle mouthpiece, its tone being soft and mournful (cf. *Ham.* 3. 2.); 5. 1. 123

RERE-MOUSE, bat; 2. 2. 4

RESPECT (in my), as far as I am concerned; 2. 1. 224

RESPECT (vb.) regard; 1. 1. 160; 5. 1. 92

RHEUMATIC DISEASES, i.e. diseases affecting the 'rheum,' including catarrhs, and colds of all kinds; 2. 1. 105

RID, (a) ridden, (b) rid himself of, discharged; 5. 1. 119

RINGLET, a circular dance, a fairy-ring (cf. Drayton, *Quest of Cynthia*, 'When Fayries in their Ringlets there/Do daunce their nightly rounds'); 2. 1. 86

RIPE, ready, prepared; 5. 1. 42

ROTE (by), from memory; 5. 1. 395

ROUND, ROUNDEL, (i) 'The simplest form of country dance is that in which the dancers form a circle; this was called a Round or Roundel' (*Sh. Eng.* ii. 440); 2. 1. 140; 2. 2. 1; (ii) 'about a round,' i.e. a roundabout course; 3. 1. 101

RUSSET, red or (sometimes) grey; 3. 2. 21

SANDED, sandy-coloured; 4. 1. 119

SCRIP, a piece of writing. It is tempting to suppose that 'the scrip' was a technical name for the theatrical 'Names of all the Actors,' together with the names of those playing them, which the Folio printers seem to have availed themselves of for certain plays; O.E.D., curiously enough, does not quote any example of 'scrip' before 1617; 1. 2. 3

SET AGAINST, oppose; 3. 2. 146

SHREWD, (i) mischievous; 2. 1. 33; (ii) shrewish; 3. 2. 323

SIMPLICITY, harmlessness (cf. *Matt.* x. 16); 1. 1. 171

SINCE, 'since night' = a night ago; 3. 2. 275

SKILL, knowledge, science; 2. 2. 127

SNUFF (in), (a) in need of snuffing, (b) in a rage; 5. 1. 248

SOJOURN TO, travel to (v. O.E.D. 'sojourn' 4); 3. 2. 171

SORT, (i) set, crew; 3. 2. 13; (ii) 'in sort' = in company, assembled together; 3. 2. 21; (iii) rank; 3. 2. 159

SPHERE, one of 'the concentric, transparent, hollow globes imagined by the older astronomers as revolving round the earth and respectively carrying with them the several heavenly bodies' O.E.D.; 2. 1. 7, 153; 3. 2. 61

SPLEEN, a sudden access of passion; 1. 1. 146

SPLIT (to make all), i.e. with agony or laughter. Cf. Greene, *Never too late* (1590), 'With that he set downe his period with such a sigh, that as the Marriners say, a man would have thought all would have split again'; 1. 2. 26

SPOTTED, wicked, morally stained; 1. 1. 110

SPRING, beginning; 2. 1. 82

SQUARE, quarrel; 2. 1. 30

SQUASH, the unripe pod of a pea; 3. 1. 177

STOP (the), an expression from the manège meaning 'a sudden check in a horse's career'; 5. 1. 120

STREAK, smear; 2. 1. 257

TAILOR, meaning uncertain, variously explained thus: (i) 'he that slips beside his chair falls as a tailor squats upon his board' Johnson; (ii) a corruption of 'tailard,' an opprobrious epithet meaning 'one with a tail,' v. O.E.D.; (iii) Furness suggests 'tailer' on the analogy of 'header.' The second interpretation seems the most likely; 2. 1. 54

TAWNY tanned (cf. *orange-tawny*); 3. 2. 263

TEAR A CAT, 'to play the part of a roistering hero' O.E.D. Cf.

Day, *Isle of Gulls*, 'a whole play of such teare-cat thunder-claps;' 1. 2. 25

THISNE, or thissen=in this manner. A dialect word of the North and Midlands; 1. 2. 48

THRUM, the tufted end of a weaver's warp; 5. 1. 284

TIRING-HOUSE, the attiring-house, or green-room of the Elizabethan theatre; 3. 1. 4

TONGS, a rude musical instrument played with a 'key' like the triangle; 4. 1. 29

TOUCH, exploit; 3. 2. 70

TRANSLATED, transformed; 1. 1. 191; 3. 1. 114; 3. 2. 32

TUNEABLE, musical; 1. 1. 184

TWO OF THE FIRST. In heraldry 'the first'=the colour first mentioned in blazoning a coat of arms; 3. 2. 213

UNBREATHED, unexercised; 'breathed'=in good wind (of a horse); 5. 1. 74

UNEVEN, crooked; 3. 2. 417

VAWARD, vanward, forepart; 4. 1. 104

VIRTUOUS, of efficacious or powerful properties; 3. 2. 367

WANTON, rank-growing; 2. 1. 99

WEED, garment; 2. 1. 256; 2. 2. 79

WELL DERIVED, well-descended; 1. 1. 99

WHOLE, solid (cf. 'whole as the marble' *Macb.* 3. 4. 22); 3. 2. 53

WOOD, mad; 2. 1. 192

WOODBINE. Prob. an error for 'bindweed'; 4. 1. 41

WRATH, wrathful, 2. 1. 20